Crocheted Dogs

Crocheted Dogs

VANESSA MOONCIE

THE GUILD OF MASTER CRAFTSMAN PUBLICATIONS

Contents

Introduction

This book brings together a collection of 10 crocheted dog patterns. The breeds include a Chihuahua, a Border Terrier and a Labrador. The projects are designed to suit all levels, from the beginner to the experienced crocheter.

A variety of stitches are used to create the dogs. The projects are worked predominantly in rounds and rows of double crochet stitch. Half treble and treble stitches are used to shape the French Bulldog's face and a few of the dogs' tails. Loop stitch is used for the Spaniel's ears and coat, and on the tails of the German Shepherd and the Yorkshire Terrier. The curly coat of the Poodle is formed by crocheting loops of chain stitch. The markings of the Dachshund and the German Shepherd are created by working with multiple colours. All of the projects are crocheted in double-knit yarn. The written instructions are accompanied by charts to make it easy to follow the patterns.

At the back of the book there are tips on getting started and illustrated step-by-step instructions for the crochet stitches used in the patterns. There are also tips on joining in colours, stuffing the dogs and adding the finishing touches, including the embroidery stitches that are used for the eyes and noses, as well as other features, such as the Dalmatian's spots. Choose the colours to match your own dog and add any distinctive markings with embroidery to create a unique portrait of your family pet. These soft toys will make a wonderful gift for dog lovers of all ages.

Vanessa Mooncie

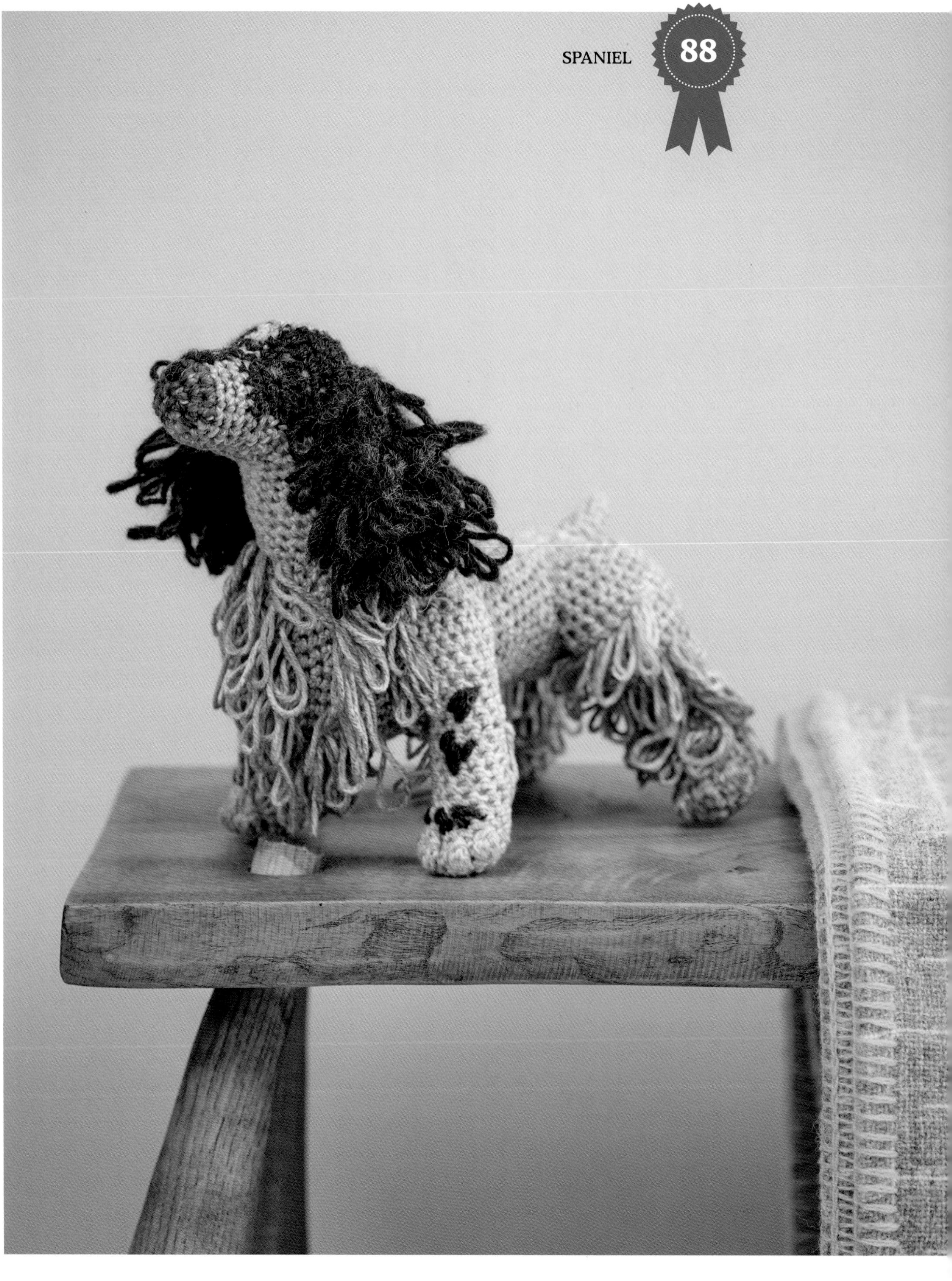

Dachshund

THE BLACK AND TAN MARKINGS ON THE DACHSHUND'S MUZZLE ARE FORMED BY CROCHETING IN ROWS, CARRYING THE UNUSED YARN ACROSS THE WRONG SIDE OF THE WORK. APART FROM THE TAIL AND EARS, THE REST OF THIS SAUSAGE DOG IS WORKED IN CONTINUOUS ROUNDS.

Materials

- Cascade 220 Superwash, 100% superwash wool (220yd/200m per 100g ball), or any DK yarn:
  1 x 100g ball in 297 Copper Heather (A)
  1 x 100g ball in 1913 Jet (B)
- Approximately 15in (38cm) length of brown DK yarn, such as 819 Chocolate (C)
- 3.25mm (UK10:USD/3) crochet hook
- Blunt-ended yarn needle
- Toy stuffing

Size

- Approximately 9⅞in (25cm) body length from tip of nose to back of hind legs
- Approximately 6¾in (17cm) tall from top of head

Tension

22 sts and 24 rows to 4in (10cm) over double crochet using 3.25mm hook. Use larger or smaller hook if necessary to obtain correct tension.

Method

The Dachshund's body and legs are worked in continuous rounds of double crochet. The muzzle, head and neck are worked in one piece. The muzzle is crocheted in rows, working with two colours, and the head and neck are continued in rounds. The ears and tail are worked in rows. Double crochet, half treble and slip stitches are used to shape the tail. The long edges of the tail are sewn together and a small amount of stuffing is inserted before sewing it in place. The toes on the paws are produced by crocheting bobbles. These appear on the reverse side of the fabric, so the work is turned before continuing with the leg. The eyes, nose and markings above the eyes are embroidered in satin stitch.

1 ch at beg of the row/round does not count as a st throughout.

Head

Starting at front of muzzle, with 3.25mm hook and A, make a magic loop (see page 145).

Round 1: 1 ch, 6 dc into loop (6 sts).
Round 2 (inc): (Dc2inc) 6 times. Join B in last dc, turn (12 sts). Pull tightly on short end of yarn to close loop.

FACE

The following is worked in rows. Carry unused yarn across the WS of the work (see page 149).

Row 1 (WS): With B, work 1 ch, 1 dc in next 2 dc; with A, work 1 dc in next 10 dc, sl st in next st, turn.
Row 2 (RS): With A, work 1 dc in next 10 dc; with B, work 1 dc in next 2 dc, turn.
Row 3: Rep row 1.
Row 4 (inc): With A, (3 dc, dc2inc) twice, 1 dc in next 2 dc; with B, work 1 dc in next dc, dc2inc, turn (15 sts).

HEAD
ROUNDS 1–2

Row 5: With B, work 1 ch, 1 dc in next 3 dc; with A, work 1 dc in next 12 dc, sl st in next st, turn.
Row 6 (inc): With A, work (4 dc, dc2inc) twice, 1 dc in next 2 dc; with B, work 1 dc in next 2 dc, dc2inc, turn (18 sts).
Row 7: With B, work 1 ch, 1 dc in next 6 dc; with A, work 1 dc in next 10 dc; with B, work 1 dc in next 2 dc, sl st in next st, turn.
Row 8 (inc): With B, 1 dc in next 2 dc; with A, work 1 dc in next 3 dc, dc2inc, 1 dc in next 5 dc, dc2inc; with B, work 1 dc in next 5 dc, dc2inc, turn (21 sts).
Row 9: With B, work 1 ch, 1 dc in next 8 dc; with A, work 1 dc in next 10 dc; with B, work 1 dc in next 3 dc, sl st in next st, turn.
Row 10: With B, 1 dc in next 4 dc; with A, work 1 dc in next 8 dc; with B, work 1 dc in next 9 dc, turn.
Row 11: With B, work 1 ch, 1 dc in next 10 dc; with A, work 1 dc in next 6 dc; with B, work 1 dc in next 5 dc, sl st in next st, turn.

KEY

⊙ MAGIC LOOP	✕ DC2INC
⌒ CHAIN (CH)	✕ DC2TOG
• SLIP STITCH (SL ST)	⊤ HALF TREBLE (HTR)
+ DOUBLE CROCHET (DC)	⊕ MAKE BOBBLE (MB)

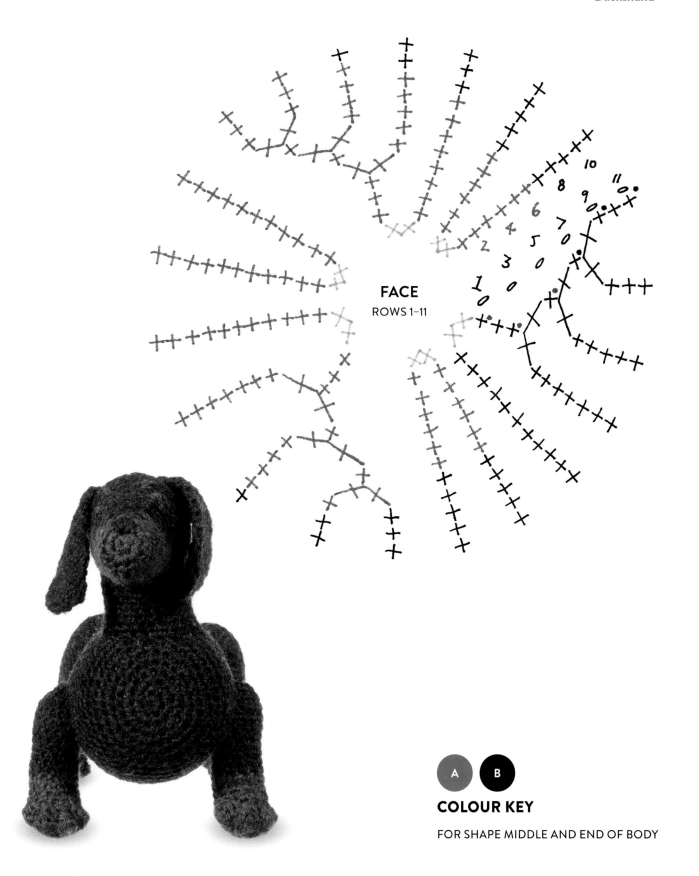

FACE
ROWS 1–11

COLOUR KEY

FOR SHAPE MIDDLE AND END OF BODY

DIVIDE FOR NECK

Fasten off A and continue with yarn B. The following is worked in rounds.

Round 1: 1 dc in next 5 dc, 15 ch, skip next 6 dc, 1 dc in next 10 dc.

Round 2 (inc): 1 dc in next 5 dc, 1 dc in next 15 ch, 1 dc in next 5 dc, (dc2inc) 5 times (35 sts).

TOP OF HEAD

Round 3 (dec): 1 dc in next 5 dc, (dc2tog, 1 dc) 5 times, 1 dc in next 15 dc (30 sts).

Round 4: 1 dc in each dc.

Round 5 (dec): (Dc2tog, 3 dc) 6 times (24 sts).

Round 6 (dec): (Dc2tog, 2 dc) 6 times (18 sts).

Round 7 (dec): (Dc2tog, 1 dc) 6 times (12 sts).

Round 8 (dec): (Dc2tog) 6 times (6 sts).

Break yarn and thread through last round of stitches. Pull tightly on end of yarn to close. Fasten off.

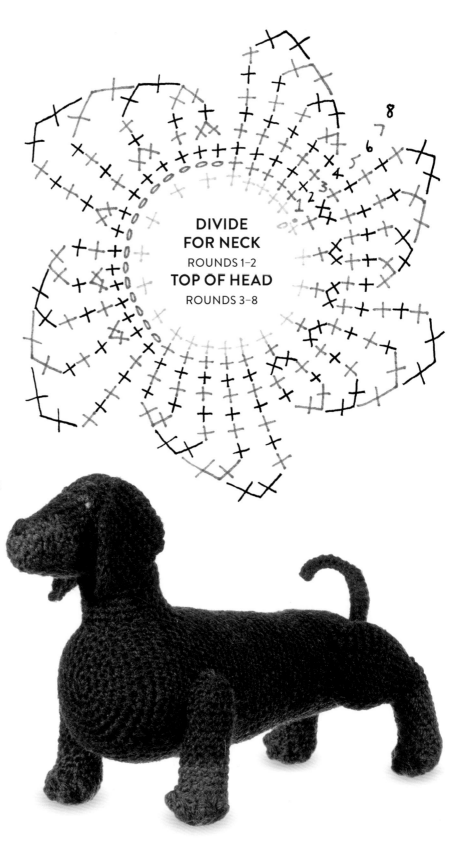

DIVIDE FOR NECK
ROUNDS 1–2
TOP OF HEAD
ROUNDS 3–8

NECK

With RS of head facing, 3.25mm hook and B, sl st in first of skipped 6 dc.

Round 1: 1 dc in same st as sl st, 1 dc in next 5 dc, 1 dc in reverse side of next 15 ch (21 sts).

Rounds 2–4: 1 dc in each dc.

Round 5: (Dc2inc, 6 dc) 3 times (24 sts).

Rounds 6–8: 1 dc in each dc. Sl st in next st and fasten off, leaving a long tail of yarn at the end.

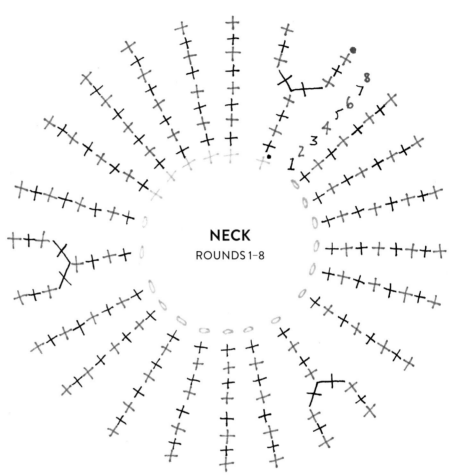

NECK
ROUNDS 1–8

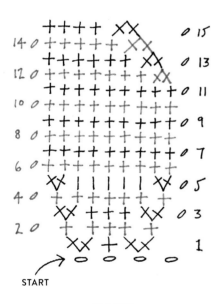

START

EARS
ROWS 1–15

Ears (make 2)

With 3.25mm hook and B, make 4 ch.

Row 1 (inc): 2 dc in 2nd ch from hook, 1 dc in next ch, 2 dc in end ch, turn (5 sts).

Row 2: 1 ch, 1 dc in each dc, turn.

Row 3 (inc): 1 ch, dc2inc, 1 dc in each dc to last st, dc2inc, turn (7 sts).

Rows 4–5: Rep last 2 rows (9 sts).

Rows 6–11: 1 ch, 1 dc in each dc, turn.

Row 12 (dec): 1 ch, 1 dc in each dc to last 2 sts, dc2tog, turn (8 sts).

Row 13 (dec): 1 ch, dc2tog, 1 dc in each dc to end, turn (7 sts).

Rows 14–15 (dec): Rep last 2 rows (5 sts).

Fasten off, leaving a long tail of yarn at the end.

Body

Starting at front of body, with
3.25mm hook and B, make a magic
loop.

Round 1: 1 ch, 6 dc into loop (6 sts).

Round 2 (inc): (Dc2inc) 6 times
(12 sts). Pull tightly on short end
of yarn to close loop.

Round 3 (inc): (Dc2inc, 1 dc)
6 times (18 sts).

Round 4 (inc): (Dc2inc, 2 dc)
6 times (24 sts).

Rounds 5–7: Continue increasing
6 sts on each round as set until there
are 42 sts.

Rounds 8–25: 1 dc in each dc.
Stuff body to within the last few
rounds before continuing.

Round 26 (dec): (Dc2tog, 5 dc)
6 times (36 sts).

Rounds 27–36: 1 dc in each dc.

Round 37 (dec): (Dc2tog, 4 dc)
6 times (30 sts).
Insert more stuffing to within the
last few rounds before continuing.

Rounds 38–52: 1 dc in each dc.
Add more stuffing before
continuing.

Rounds 53–56: Work as for rounds
5–8 of top of head (6 sts).
Break yarn and thread through last
round of stitches. Pull tightly on end
of yarn to close. Fasten off.

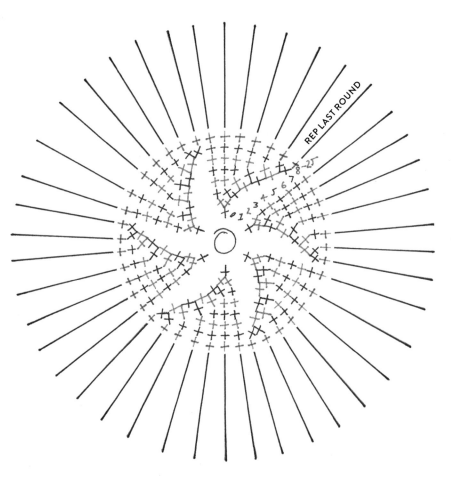

BODY
ROUNDS 1–25

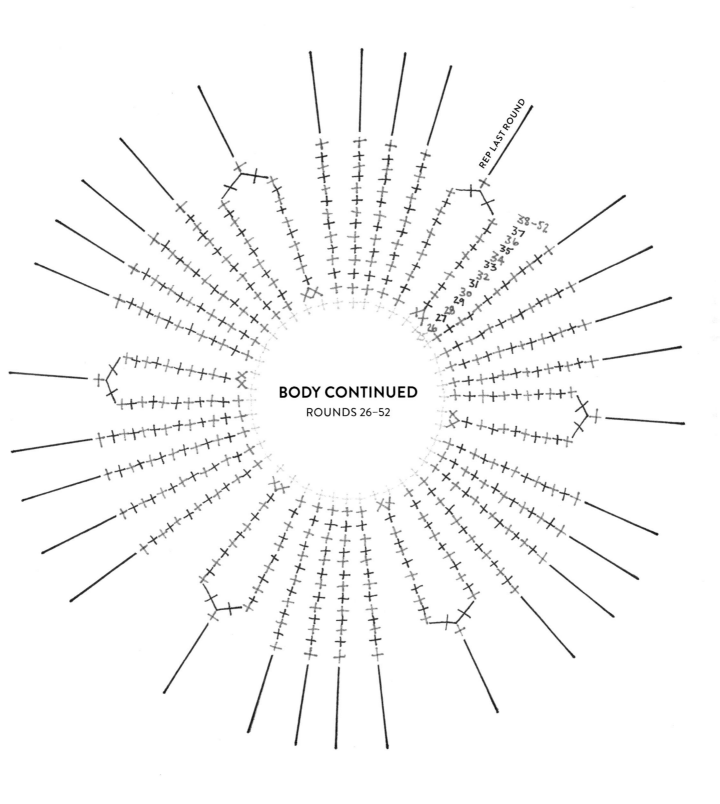

BODY CONTINUED
ROUNDS 26–52

Front legs (make 2)

The bobbles appear on the reverse side of the work. This will be the right side. See page 148 for the instructions to make bobble (mb). Starting at the base of the paw, with 3.25mm hook and A, make a magic loop.

Round 1 (WS): 1 ch, 6 dc into loop (6 sts).

Round 2 (inc): (Dc2inc) 6 times (12 sts). Pull tightly on short end of yarn to close loop.

Round 3 (inc): (Dc2inc, 2 dc) 4 times (16 sts).

Round 4: 1 dc in next 8 dc, (mb, 1 dc in next dc) 4 times, turn.

Round 5 (RS) (dec): 1 ch, 1 dc in first dc, (1 dc in next dc, dc2tog) twice, 1 dc in next 9 dc (14 sts).

Round 6 (dec): (1 dc in next dc, dc2tog) twice, 1 dc in next 8 dc (12 sts).

Rounds 7–8: 1 dc in each dc. Join B in last dc.

Fasten off A and continue with B.

Rounds 9–12: 1 dc in each dc.

Round 13 (inc): (Dc2inc, 3 dc) 3 times (15 sts).

Round 14: 1 dc in each dc.

Round 15 (inc): (Dc2inc, 4 dc) 3 times (18 sts).

Round 16: 1 dc in each dc. Stuff leg before continuing.

Round 17 (dec): (Dc2tog, 1 dc) 6 times (12 sts).

Round 18 (dec): (Dc2tog) 6 times (6 sts).

Break yarn and thread through last round of stitches. Pull tightly on end of yarn to close. Fasten off, leaving a long tail of yarn at the end.

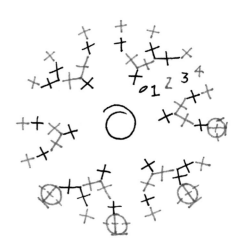

FRONT LEGS
ROUNDS 1–4

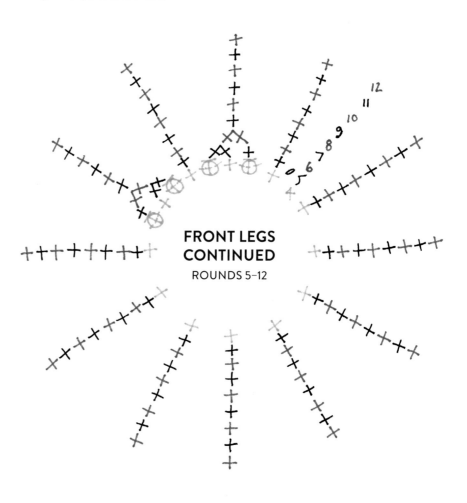

**FRONT LEGS
CONTINUED**
ROUNDS 5–12

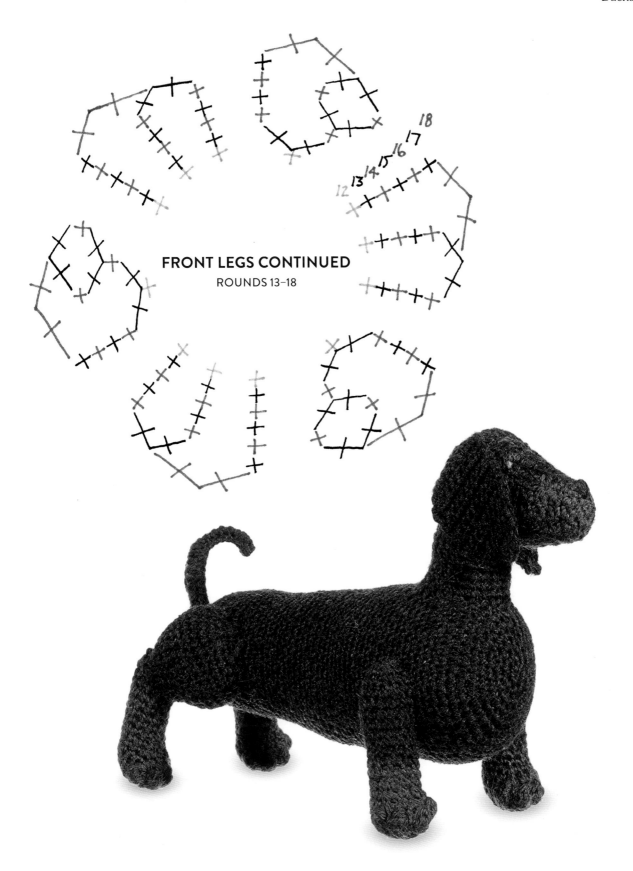

FRONT LEGS CONTINUED
ROUNDS 13–18

12 13 14 15 16 17 18

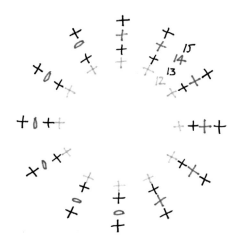

HIND LEGS
FOR ROUNDS 7–12, FOLLOW
CHARTS FOR FRONT LEGS
(SEE PAGE 26)
ROUND 13
SHAPE BACK OF LEG
ROUNDS 14–15

SHAPE BACK OF LEG

Round 14: 1 dc in next 2 dc, ending at the side of the leg; 6 ch, skip the 6 dc at the front of the leg, 1 dc in next 4 dc.

Round 15: 1 dc in next 2 dc, 1 dc in next 6 ch, 1 dc in next 4 dc. Break yarn and thread through last round of stitches. Pull tightly on end of yarn to close and fasten off.

SHAPE THIGH

With RS of leg facing, 3.25mm hook and B, sl st in first of skipped 6 dc.

Round 1: 1 dc in same st as sl st, 1 dc in next 5 dc, 1 dc in reverse side of next 6 ch (12 sts).

Round 2 (inc): (Dc2inc, 1 dc) 6 times (18 sts).

Rounds 3–4: 1 dc in each dc.

Round 5 (inc): 1 dc in next 2 dc, (dc2inc) 6 times, 1 dc in next 10 dc (24 sts).

Round 6: 1 dc in each dc.

Round 7 (inc): (Dc2inc, 3 dc) 6 times (30 sts).

Rounds 8–9: 1 dc in each dc.

Round 10 (dec): (Dc2tog, 3 dc) 6 times (24 sts).

Round 11 (dec): (Dc2tog, 2 dc) 6 times (18 sts).

Stuff leg before continuing.

Round 12 (dec): (Dc2tog, 1 dc) 6 times (12 sts).

Round 13 (dec): (Dc2tog) 6 times (6 sts).

Break yarn and thread through last round of stitches. Pull tightly on end of yarn to close. Fasten off, leaving a long tail of yarn at the end.

Hind legs (make 2)

Starting at the base of the paw, with 3.25mm hook and A, make a magic loop.

Rounds 1–6: Work as for rounds 1–6 of front legs.

Rounds 7–12: 1 dc in each dc. Join B in last dc.

Fasten off A and continue with B.

Round 13: 1 dc in each dc.

**HIND LEGS
CONTINUED**
SHAPE THIGH
ROUNDS 1–13

Tail

With 3.25mm hook and B,
make 19 ch.

Row 1: 1 dc in 2nd ch from hook,
1 dc in next 7 ch, 1 htr in next 10 ch,
turn (18 sts).

Row 2: 2 ch (does not count as a st),
1 htr in next 10 htr, 1 dc in next 4 dc,
sl st in next 4 dc. Fasten off, leaving
a long tail of yarn at the end.

TAIL
ROWS 1–2

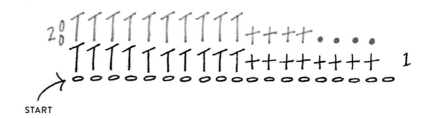

Making up

HEAD

Stuff the head. Use the tail of yarn
left after fastening off to sew the
head to the body, stitching all
around the neck. Insert more
stuffing into the neck if necessary.
In satin stitch (see page 152),
embroider eyes with yarn C, nose
with B and the markings above the
eyes with yarn A.

EARS

Positioning the ears so the
decreased stitches of the last few
rows are at the lower edges, pin an
ear in place to each side of the
head. Turn back the ear so it is
pointing up and sew in place along
the 5 stitches of the last row. Fold
the ears down. To set the ears in
place, dampen them and stick a pin
through each ear and into the neck
to hold them in shape. Remove the
pins when the ears are dry.

LEGS

Flatten the top of the legs and sew
in place, stitching around the tops of
the thighs.

TAIL

Using the length of yarn left after
fastening off, fold the tail lengthways
and sew the long edges together
with whip stitch (see page 151).
The tail will have a natural curve
to it. Use the end of the crochet
hook to push a small amount of
stuffing into the wide end of the
tail. Sew the tail in place. Weave
in the short ends of yarn.

Border Terrier

THE TWEED YARN GIVES THE EFFECT OF THE BORDER TERRIER'S COARSE COAT.
THE WHISKERS ARE MADE BY ATTACHING STRANDS OF YARN TO THE STITCHES
OF THE MUZZLE, THEN SEPARATING THE FIBRES AND TRIMMING THEM TO SHAPE.

Materials

- Rowan Hemp Tweed, 75% wool, 25% true hemp (104yd/95m per 50g ball), or any DK yarn:
  1 x 50g ball in 136 Granite (A)
  2 x 50g balls in 140 Cameo (B)
- Approximately 20in (51cm) length of black DK yarn, such as Rowan Pure Wool Superwash in 198 Caviar (C)
- 3.25mm (UK10:USD/3) crochet hook
- Blunt-ended yarn needle
- Toy stuffing

Size

- Approximately 8¼in (21cm) body length from tip of nose to back of hind legs
- Approximately 7½in (19cm) tall from top of head

Tension

20 sts and 22 rows to 4in (10cm) over double crochet using 3.25mm hook and yarn A. Use larger or smaller hook if necessary to obtain correct tension.

Method

The Border Terrier's body and legs are worked in continuous rounds of double crochet. The muzzle, head and neck are worked in one piece. The front of the head is crocheted in rounds and the top of the head is worked in rows. The neck is crocheted in rounds, first crocheting into the stitches at the underside of the muzzle, and then along the edges of the rows that make up the top of the head. The ears and tail are worked in rows. Double crochet, half treble and slip stitches form the tapered shape of the tail. The long edges of the tail are sewn together and a small amount of stuffing is inserted before sewing it in place. The toes on the paws are produced by crocheting bobbles. The bobbles on the paws appear on the reverse side of the fabric. The eyes and nose are embroidered in black yarn. To make the whiskers, folded strands of yarn are threaded around the stitches of the muzzle, passing the ends through the loop and pulling tight to secure them. The fibres are separated with a pin to fluff them up before trimming them to shape.

1 ch at beg of the row/round does not count as a st throughout.

Body

HEAD

Starting at front of muzzle, with 3.25mm hook and A, make a magic loop (see page 145).

Round 1: 1 ch, 5 dc into loop (5 sts).

Round 2 (inc): (Dc2inc) 5 times (10 sts). Pull tightly on short end of yarn to close loop.

Round 3: (Dc2inc, 1 dc) 5 times (15 sts).

Rounds 4–5: 1 dc in each dc. Join B in last dc.

Continue with B.

Round 6: 1 dc in each dc.

Round 7 (inc): (Dc2inc, 4 dc) 3 times (18 sts).

Round 8 (inc): 1 dc in next dc, (dc2inc, 1 dc) 6 times, 1 dc in next 5 dc (24 sts).

Round 9 (inc): 1 dc in next 3 dc, (dc2inc, 2 dc) 5 times, 1 dc in next dc, finishing 5 sts before the end, turn (29 sts).

TOP OF HEAD

Row 1 (WS): 1 ch, 1 dc in next 24 dc, turn.

Continue on these 24 sts.

Rows 2–5: 1 ch, 1 dc in each dc, turn. Place a marker in the centre of row 5.

Row 6 (WS) (dec): 1 ch, (dc2tog, 2 dc) 6 times, turn (18 sts).

Row 7 (dec): 1 ch, (dc2tog, 1 dc) 6 times, turn (12 sts).

Row 8 (dec): 1 ch, (dc2tog) 6 times (6 sts).

Break yarn and thread through last 6 stitches. Pull tightly on end of yarn. Fasten off.

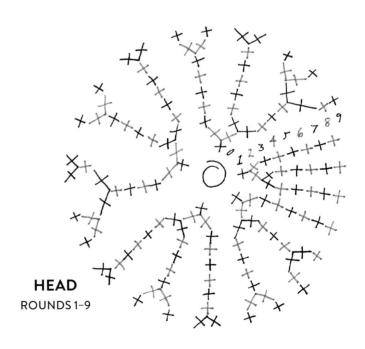

HEAD
ROUNDS 1–9

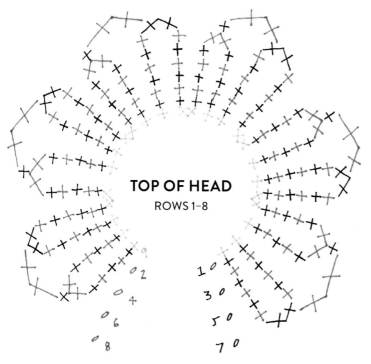

TOP OF HEAD
ROWS 1–8

NECK

With RS of head facing, 3.25mm hook and B, sl st in first of unworked 5 dc of round 9 of head.

Round 1: 1 dc in same st as sl st, 1 dc in next 4 dc, work 14 dc evenly along edge of the rows of head (19 sts).

Rounds 2–6: Dc in each dc.

Round 7: (Dc2inc, 1 dc) 5 times, 1 dc in next 9 dc (24 sts).

Round 8: Dc in each dc.

Round 9: 1 dc in next 13 dc. Sl st in next st and fasten off, leaving a long tail of yarn at the end.

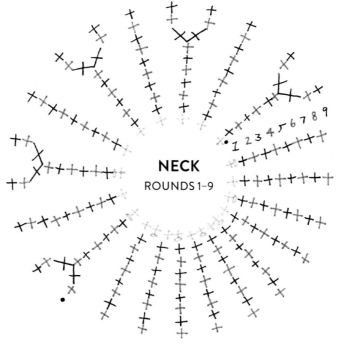

NECK
ROUNDS 1–9

KEY

◠	MAGIC LOOP	✕✕	DC2INC
⌀	CHAIN (CH)	✕✕	DC2TOG
•	SLIP STITCH (SL ST)	⊤	HALF TREBLE (HTR)
+	DOUBLE CROCHET (DC)	⊕	MAKE BOBBLE (MB)

Ears (make 2)

Starting at the tip of the ear, with 3.25mm hook and A, make 2 ch.

Row 1 (inc): 2 dc in 2nd ch from hook, turn (2 sts).

Rows 2–5 (inc): 1 ch, dc2inc, 1 dc in each dc to end, turn (6 sts).

Rows 6–8: 1 ch, 1 dc in each dc.

SHAPE LOWER EDGE

Row 9 (dec): 1 ch, (dc2tog) twice, turn.

Continue on these 2 sts.

Row 10 (dec): 1 ch, dc2tog (1 st).

Fasten off, leaving a long tail of yarn at the end.

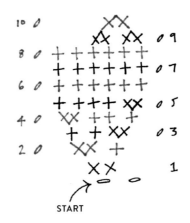

EARS
ROWS 1–10

Body

Starting at front of body, with 3.25mm hook and B, make 10 ch.

Round 1: 1 dc in 2nd ch from hook, 1 dc in next 7 ch, 2 dc in end ch, 1 dc in reverse side of next 8 ch. Place a marker on the first stitch to mark the top of the front of the body (18 sts).

Round 2 (inc): (Dc2inc, 2 dc) 6 times (24 sts).

Round 3 (inc): (Dc2inc, 3 dc) 6 times (30 sts).

Round 4 (inc): (Dc2inc, 4 dc) 6 times (36 sts).

Rounds 5–17: 1 dc in each dc.

Round 18 (dec): (Dc2tog, 4 dc) 6 times (30 sts).

Rounds 19–23: 1 dc in each dc.

Round 24 (dec): (Dc2tog, 3 dc) 6 times (24 sts).

Rounds 25–32: 1 dc in each dc. Stuff body before continuing.

Round 33 (dec): (Dc2tog, 2 dc) 6 times (18 sts).

Round 34 (dec): (Dc2tog, 1 dc) 6 times (12 sts).

Round 35 (dec): (Dc2tog) 6 times (6 sts).

Break yarn and thread through last 6 stitches. Pull tightly on end of yarn to close. Fasten off.

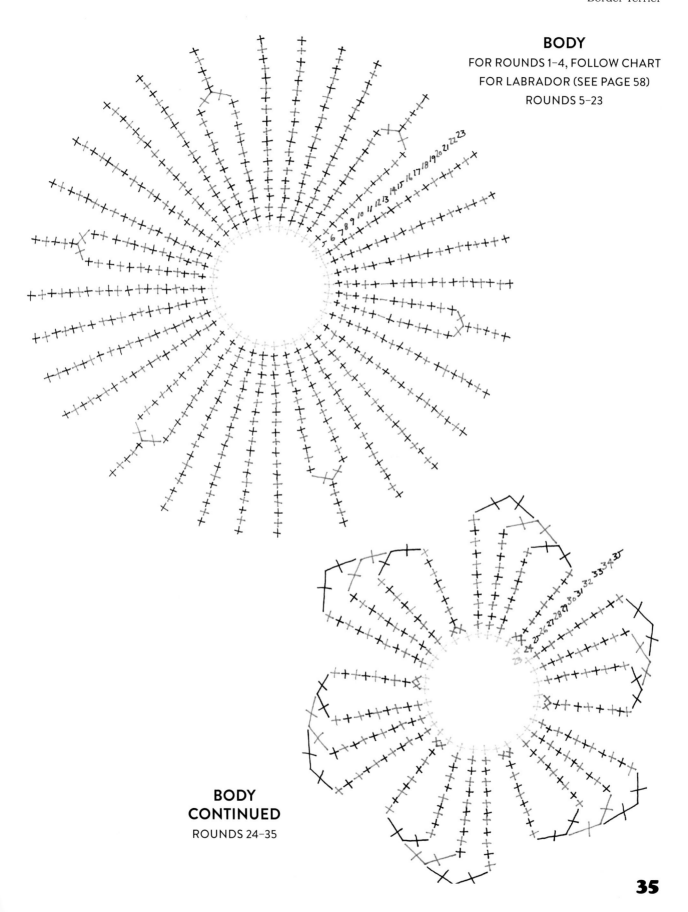

BODY
FOR ROUNDS 1–4, FOLLOW CHART
FOR LABRADOR (SEE PAGE 58)
ROUNDS 5–23

**BODY
CONTINUED**
ROUNDS 24–35

Front legs (make 2)

The bobbles appear on the reverse side of the work. This will be the right side. See page 148 for instructions to make bobble (mb). Starting at the base of the paw, with 3.25mm hook and B, make a magic loop.

Round 1 (WS): 1 ch, 6 dc into loop (6 sts).

Round 2 (inc): (Dc2inc) 6 times (12 sts). Pull tightly on short end of yarn to close loop.

Round 3 (inc): (Dc2inc, 2 dc) 4 times (16 sts).

Round 4: 1 dc in next 8 dc, (mb, 1 dc in next dc) 4 times, turn.

Round 5 (RS) (dec): 1 ch, 1 dc in first dc, (1 dc in next st, dc2tog) twice, 1 dc in next 9 dc (14 sts).

Round 6 (dec): (1 dc in next dc, dc2tog) twice, 1 dc in next 8 dc (12 sts).

Rounds 7–17: 1 dc in each dc.

Round 18 (inc): (Dc2inc, 3 dc) 3 times (15 sts).

Rounds 19–23: 1 dc in each dc. Stuff leg before continuing.

Round 24 (dec): (Dc2tog, 1 dc) 5 times (10 sts).

Round 25 (dec): (Dc2tog) 5 times (5 sts).

Break yarn and thread through last round of stitches. Pull tightly on end of yarn to close. Fasten off, leaving a long tail of yarn at the end.

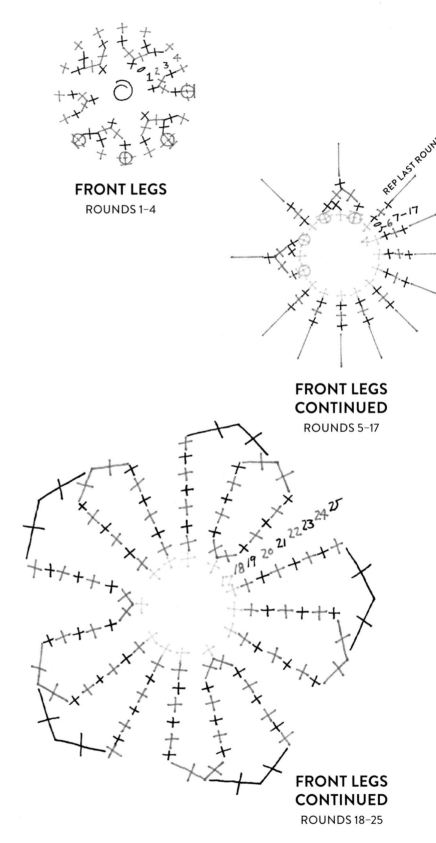

FRONT LEGS
ROUNDS 1–4

FRONT LEGS CONTINUED
ROUNDS 5–17

FRONT LEGS CONTINUED
ROUNDS 18–25

Hind legs (make 2)

Starting at the base of the paw, with 3.25mm hook and B, make a magic loop.

Rounds 1–12: Work as for rounds 1–12 of front legs.

HIND LEGS
SHAPE BACK OF LEG
ROUNDS 13–14

SHAPE BACK OF LEG

Round 13: 1 dc in next dc, ending at the side of the leg; 6 ch, skip the 6 dc at the front of the leg, 1 dc in next 5 dc.

Round 14: 1 dc in next dc, 1 dc in next 6 ch, 1 dc in next 5 dc. Break yarn and thread through last round of stitches. Pull tightly on end of yarn to close and fasten off.

SHAPE THIGH

With RS of leg facing, 3.25mm hook and B, sl st in first of skipped 6 dc of round 12.

Round 1: 1 dc in same st as sl st, 1 dc in next 5 dc, 1 dc in reverse side of next 6 ch (12 sts).

Rounds 2–5: 1 dc in each dc.

Round 6 (inc): (Dc2inc, 3 dc) 3 times (15 sts).

Round 7: 1 dc in each dc.

Round 8 (inc): (Dc2inc, 4 dc) 3 times (18 sts).

Round 9: 1 dc in each dc.

Round 10 (inc): (Dc2inc, 5 dc) 3 times (21 sts).

Round 11: 1 dc in each dc.

Round 12 (inc): (Dc2inc, 6 dc) 3 times (24 sts).

Rounds 13–14: 1 dc in each dc. Stuff leg before continuing.

Round 15 (dec): (Dc2tog, 2 dc) 6 times (18 sts).

Round 16 (dec): (Dc2tog, 1 dc) 6 times (12 sts).

Round 17 (dec): (Dc2tog) 6 times (6 sts). Break yarn and thread through last round of stitches. Pull tightly on end of yarn to close. Fasten off, leaving a long tail of yarn at the end.

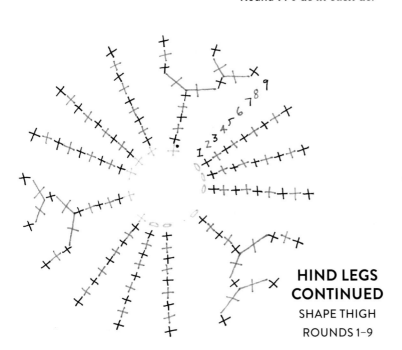

HIND LEGS CONTINUED
SHAPE THIGH
ROUNDS 1–9

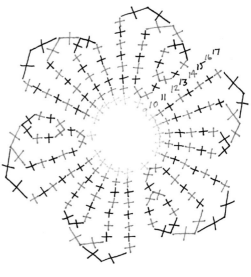

HIND LEGS CONTINUED
SHAPE THIGH
ROUNDS 10–17

Tail

With 3.25mm hook and B, make 13 ch.

Row 1: 1 dc in 2nd ch from hook, 1 dc in next 8 ch, 1 htr in next 3 ch, turn (12 sts).

Row 2: 1 ch, 1 dc in each st, turn.

Row 3: 1 ch, 1 dc in next 9 dc, 1 htr in next 3 dc, turn.

Row 4: 1 ch, 1 dc in next 9 sts, sl st in next 3 dc.

Fasten off, leaving a long tail of yarn at the end.

TAIL
ROWS 1–4

Making up

HEAD
Stuff the head. With the tail of yarn left after fastening off, sew the head in place, indicated by the marker at the top of the body. Stitch all around the neck edges. Insert more stuffing into the neck if necessary. With C, embroider the eyes and nose in satin stitch (see page 152).

EARS
Align the edges of the ears with the row of stitches of the head, indicated by the marker, positioning the decreased edges down each side of the head. With the tips of the ears pointing towards the nose, sew the ears in place along the stitches of the shaped lower edge. Dampen down the ears. Move the tip of each ear back towards the neck. Stick a pin through the tips and then into the neck to hold the ears in position. Remove the pins when the ears are dry.

LEGS
Flatten the tops of the legs and sew in place, stitching all around the tops of the thighs.

TAIL
Using the length of yarn left after fastening off, fold the tail lengthways and sew the long edges together with whip stitch (see page 151). Use the end of the crochet hook to push a small amount of stuffing into the tail. Sew the tail in place. Weave in all ends.

WHISKERS
The whiskers are made with tassels (see page 153) that are threaded through the posts of the stitches. Use one 4in (10cm) length of yarn A or B for each tassel. Attach the tassels to the posts of the stitches around the first five rounds of the head. Trim the ends and use a pin to gently separate the fibres.

French Bulldog

VARIOUS STITCH LENGTHS FORM THE FRONT OF THE FRENCH BULLDOG'S
MUZZLE, USING A COMBINATION OF DOUBLE CROCHET, HALF TREBLE,
TREBLE AND SLIP STITCHES TO PRODUCE THE SHAPING.

Materials

- Rowan Pure Wool Superwash DK, 100% wool
  (137yd/125m per 50g ball), or any DK yarn:
  1 x 50g ball in 118 Granite (A)
  1 x 50g ball in 101 Chalk (B)
- Approximately 20in (51cm) length of black DK
  yarn, such as 198 Caviar (C)
- 3.25mm (UK10:USD/3) crochet hook
- Blunt-ended yarn needle
- Toy stuffing

Size

- Approximately 7in (18cm) body length from
  muzzle to back of hind legs
- Approximately 5¾in (14.5cm) tall from top of head
  (excluding ears)

Tension

22 sts and 26 rows to 4in (10cm) over double crochet
using 3.25mm hook. Use larger or smaller hook if
necessary to obtain correct tension.

Method

The French Bulldog's body, legs and tail are worked in continuous rounds of double crochet. The muzzle, head and neck are worked in one piece. The shaped part of the muzzle is worked in rows, starting in the front loops of the previous round. The top of the head is worked in rows. The neck is crocheted in rounds, first crocheting into the stitches at the underside of the muzzle, and then along the edges of the rows that make up the top of the head. The ears are worked in rows. Each ear is made with two identical pieces that are joined by crocheting into each stitch of both pieces at the same time. The toes on the paws are produced by crocheting bobbles. The bobbles on the paws appear on the reverse side of the fabric. The eyes and nose are embroidered in black yarn.

1 ch at beg of the row/round does not count as a st throughout.

Muzzle

With 3.25mm hook and A, make a magic loop (see page 145).
Round 1: 1 ch, 6 dc into loop (6 sts).
Round 2 (inc): (Dc2inc) 6 times (12 sts). Pull tightly on short end of yarn to close loop.
Round 3: (Dc2inc, 1 dc) 6 times (18 sts).

SHAPE FRONT OF MUZZLE

Row 1: Working in front loop only of each stitch, 1 dc in next 12 sts, sl st in next st, turn.
Row 2: Dc2tog, *1 htr in next dc, 1 tr in next dc, 1 htr in next dc*, sl st in next 2 dc; rep from * to *, dc2tog, turn.

MUZZLE
ROUNDS 1–3

SHAPE FRONT OF MUZZLE
ROWS 1–2

KEY

◯ MAGIC LOOP

𝒐 CHAIN (CH)

• SLIP STITCH (SL ST)

╀ DOUBLE CROCHET (DC)

✕✕ DC2INC

✕✕ DC2TOG

⊤ HALF TREBLE (HTR

𝐓 TREBLE (TR))

⊕ MAKE BOBBLE (MB)

∩ WORK INTO
 BACK LOOP ONLY

∪ WORK INTO
 FRONT LOOP ONLY

43

Head

The following is worked in rounds.

Round 1: Working in the stitches of round 3 of muzzle, 1 dc in back loop of next 13 dc, 1 dc in both loops of next 5 dc.

Round 2 (inc): (Dc2inc, 2 dc) 6 times (24 sts). Join B in last dc. Continue with B.

Round 3: 1 dc in each dc.

Round 4 (inc): (Dc2inc, 2 dc) 6 times, finishing 6 sts before the end, turn (30 sts).

TOP OF HEAD

Row 1 (WS) (inc): (Dc2inc, 3 dc) 6 times, turn (30 sts).
Continue on these 30 sts.

Rows 2–4: 1 ch, 1 dc in each dc, turn.

Row 5 (dec): (Dc2tog, 3 dc) 6 times, turn (24 sts). Place a marker in the centre of this row.

Row 6 (dec): (Dc2tog, 2 dc) 6 times, turn (18 sts).

Row 7 (dec): (Dc2tog, 1 dc) 6 times, turn (12 sts).

Row 8 (dec): (Dc2tog) 6 times, turn (6 sts).

Break yarn and thread through last 6 stitches. Pull tightly on end of yarn. Fasten off.

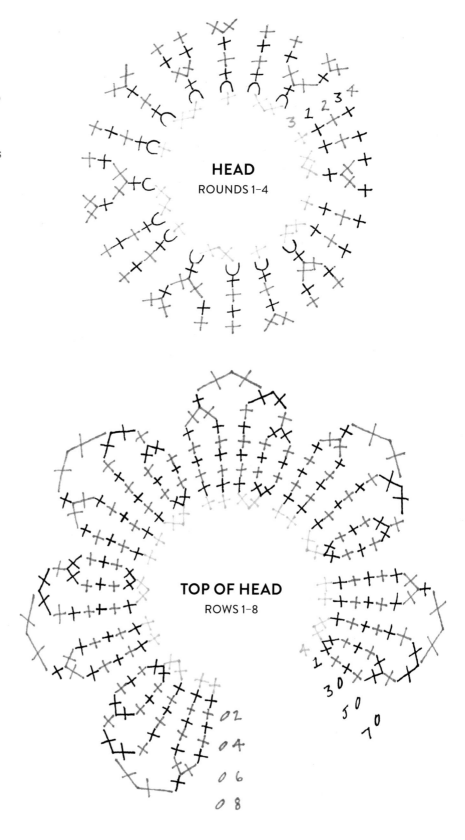

HEAD
ROUNDS 1–4

TOP OF HEAD
ROWS 1–8

NECK

With RS of head facing, 3.25mm hook and B, sl st in first of unworked 6 dc of round 4 of head.

Round 1: 1 dc in same st as sl st, 1 dc in next 5 dc, work 14 dc evenly along edge of the rows of head (20 sts).

Rounds 2–3: Dc in each dc.

Round 4: (Dc2inc, 1 dc) 4 times, 1 dc in next 12 dc (24 sts).

Rounds 5–6: Dc in each dc.

Round 7: 1 dc in next 12 dc. Sl st in next st and fasten off, leaving a long tail of yarn at the end.

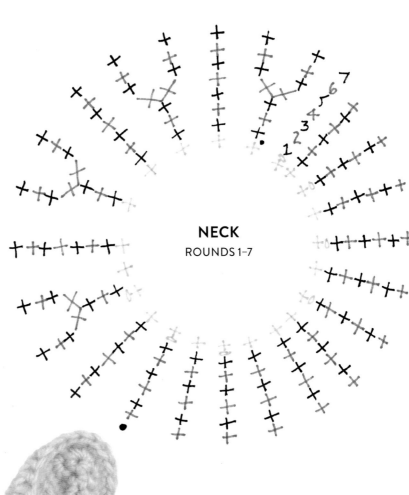

NECK
ROUNDS 1–7

Ears (make 2)

With 3.25mm hook and B,
make 6 ch.
Row 1: 1 dc in 2nd ch from hook,
1 dc in next 3 ch, 3 dc in next ch,
1 dc in reverse side of next 4 ch,
turn (11 sts).
Row 2 (inc): 1 ch, (dc2inc, 1 dc in
next 4 dc) twice, dc2inc (14 sts).
Row 3 (inc): 1 ch, (dc2inc, 1 dc in
next 5 dc, dc2inc) twice (18 sts).
Fasten off.
Make one more piece to match the
first. Turn work at the end and do
not fasten off.

JOIN EAR PIECES

Place the two ear pieces together.
Next: 1 ch, inserting the hook under
both loops of each stitch of both
pieces at the same time to join, 1 dc
in next 8 dc, (dc2inc) twice, 1 dc in
next 8 dc (20 sts). Fasten off, leaving
a long length of yarn at the end.

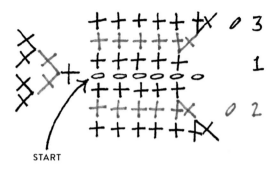

EARS
ROWS 1–3

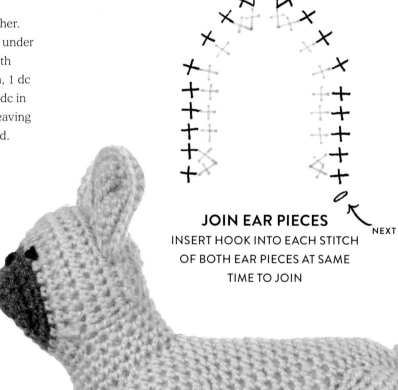

JOIN EAR PIECES
INSERT HOOK INTO EACH STITCH
OF BOTH EAR PIECES AT SAME
TIME TO JOIN

NEXT

46

Body

Starting at front of body, with 3.25mm hook and B, make a magic loop.

Round 1: 1 ch, 6 dc into loop (6 sts).

Round 2 (inc): (Dc2inc) 6 times (12 sts). Pull tightly on short end of yarn to close loop.

Round 3 (inc): (Dc2inc, 1 dc) 6 times (18 sts).

Rounds 4–7: Continue increasing 6 sts on each round as set until there are 42 sts.

Rounds 8–14: 1 dc in each dc.

Round 15 (dec): (Dc2tog, 5 dc) 6 times (36 sts).

Rounds 16–20: 1 dc in each dc.

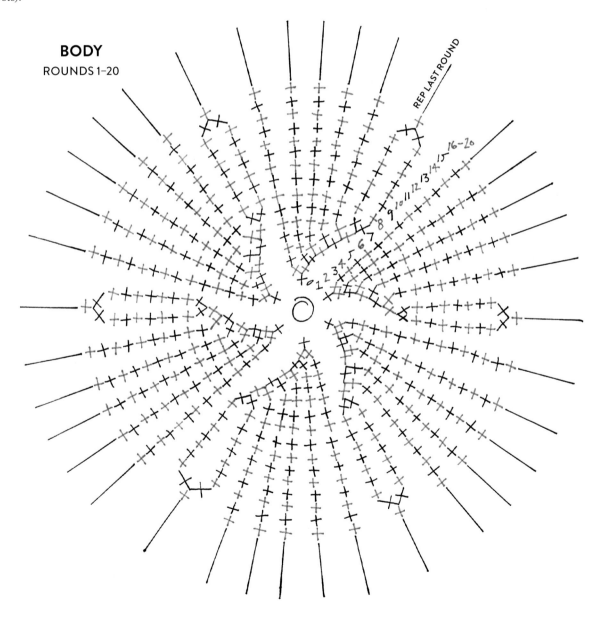

BODY
ROUNDS 1–20

Round 21 (dec): (Dc2tog, 4 dc)
6 times (30 sts).

Rounds 22–31: 1 dc in each dc.
Stuff body before continuing.

Round 32 (dec): (Dc2tog, 3 dc)
6 times (24 sts).

Round 33 (dec): (Dc2tog, 2 dc)
6 times (18 sts).

Round 34 (dec): (Dc2tog, 1 dc)
6 times (12 sts).

Round 35 (dec): (Dc2tog) 6 times
(6 sts).

Break yarn and thread through last
6 stitches. Pull tightly on end of yarn
to close. Fasten off.

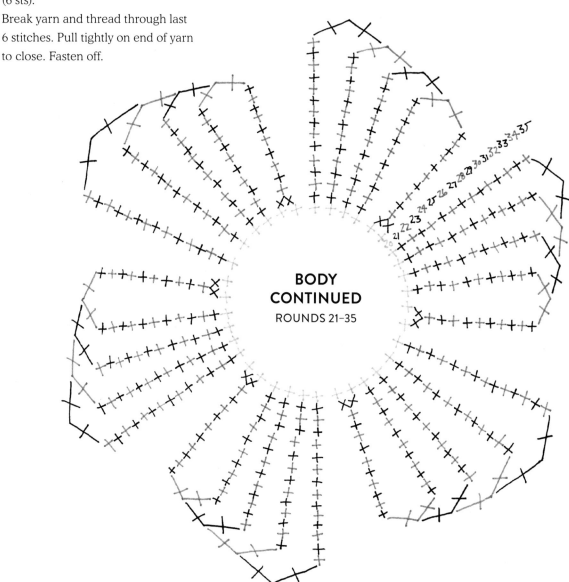

**BODY
CONTINUED**
ROUNDS 21–35

Front legs (make 2)

The bobbles appear on the reverse side of the work. This will be the right side. See page 148 for instructions to make bobble (mb). Starting at the base of the paw, with 3.25mm hook and B, make a magic loop.

Round 1 (WS): 1 ch, 6 dc into loop (6 sts).

Round 2 (inc): (Dc2inc) 6 times (12 sts). Pull tightly on short end of yarn to close loop.

Round 3 (inc): (Dc2inc, 2 dc) 4 times (16 sts).

Round 4: 1 dc in next 8 dc, (mb, 1 dc in next dc) 4 times, turn.

Round 5 (RS) (dec): 1 ch, 1 dc in first dc, (1 dc in next st, dc2tog) twice, 1 dc in next 9 dc (14 sts).

Round 6 (dec): (1 dc in next dc, dc2tog) twice, 1 dc in next 8 dc (12 sts).

Rounds 7–12: 1 dc in each dc.

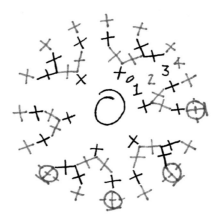

FRONT LEGS
ROUNDS 1–4

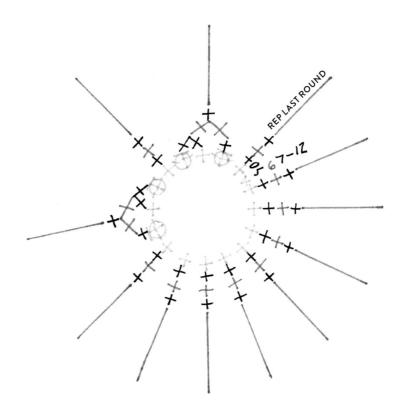

**FRONT LEGS
CONTINUED**
ROUNDS 5–12

49

Round 13 (inc): (Dc2inc, 3 dc) 3 times (15 sts).

Rounds 14–16: 1 dc in each dc.

Round 17 (inc): (Dc2inc, 4 dc) 3 times (18 sts).

Rounds 18–20: 1 dc in each dc. Stuff leg before continuing.

Round 21 (dec): (Dc2tog, 1 dc) 6 times (12 sts).

Round 22 (dec): (Dc2tog) 6 times (6 sts).

Break yarn and thread through last round of stitches. Pull tightly on end of yarn to close. Fasten off, leaving a long tail of yarn at the end.

FRONT LEGS CONTINUED
ROUNDS 13–22

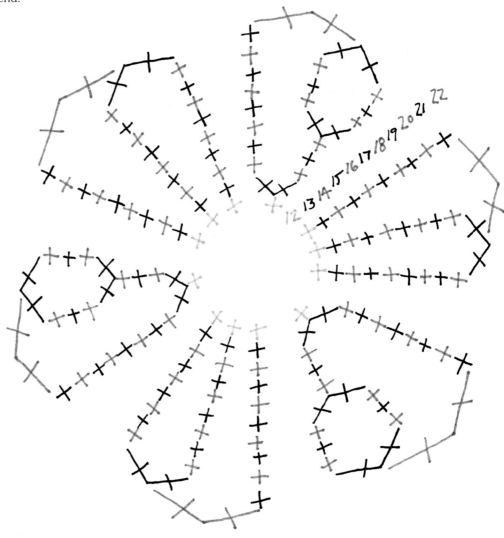

Hind legs (make 2)

Starting at the base of the paw, with 3.25mm hook and B, make a magic loop.

Rounds 1–10: Work as for rounds 1–10 of front legs.

SHAPE BACK OF LEG

Round 11: 1 dc in next dc, ending at the side of the leg; 6 ch, skip the 6 dc at the front of the leg, 1 dc in next 5 dc.

Round 12: 1 dc in next dc, 1 dc in next 6 ch, 1 dc in next 5 dc. Break yarn and thread through last round of stitches. Pull tightly on end of yarn to close and fasten off.

HIND LEGS
SHAPE BACK OF LEG
ROUNDS 11–12

SHAPE THIGH

With RS of leg facing, 3.25mm hook and B, sl st in first of skipped 6 dc of round 11.

Round 1: 1 dc in same st as sl st, 1 dc in next 5 dc, 1 dc in reverse side of next 6 ch (12 sts).

Round 2: 1 dc in each dc.

Round 3 (inc): (Dc2inc, 3 dc) 3 times (15 sts).

Round 4: 1 dc in each dc.

Round 5 (inc): (Dc2inc, 4 dc) 3 times (18 sts).

Round 6: 1 dc in each dc.

Round 7 (inc): (Dc2inc, 5 dc) 3 times (21 sts).

Round 8: 1 dc in each dc.

Round 9 (inc): (Dc2inc, 6 dc) 3 times (24 sts).

Rounds 10–13: 1 dc in each dc. Stuff leg before continuing.

Round 14 (dec): (Dc2tog, 2 dc) 6 times (18 sts).

Round 15 (dec): (Dc2tog, 1 dc) 6 times (12 sts).

Round 16 (dec): (Dc2tog) 6 times (6 sts).

Break yarn and thread through last round of stitches. Pull tightly on end of yarn to close. Fasten off, leaving a long tail of yarn at the end.

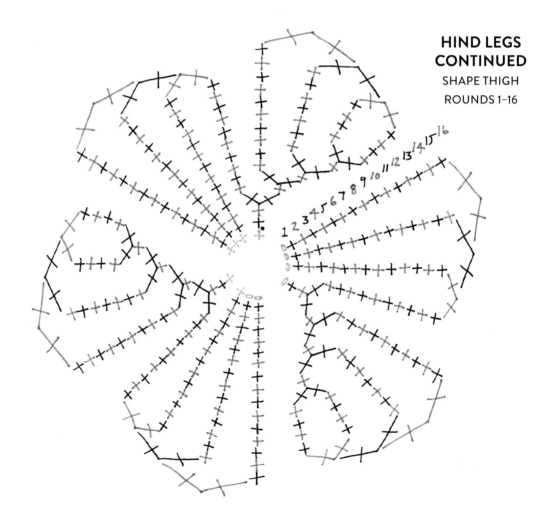

HIND LEGS CONTINUED

SHAPE THIGH

ROUNDS 1–16

Tail

Starting at tip of tail, with 3.25mm hook and B, make a magic loop.

Round 1: 1 ch, 6 dc into loop (6 sts).

Round 2: 1 dc in each dc.

Round 3 (inc): (Dc2inc, 1 dc) 3 times (9 sts). Pull tightly on short end of yarn to close loop.

Round 4: 1 dc in each dc.

Round 5 (inc): (Dc2tog, 1 dc) 3 times (6 sts).

Fasten off, leaving a long tail of yarn at the end.

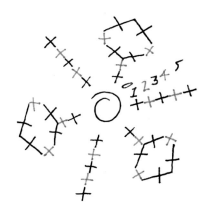

TAIL
ROUNDS 1–5

Making up

HEAD

Stuff the head. With the tail of yarn left after fastening off, sew the head to the front of the body. Stitch all around the neck edges. Insert more stuffing into the neck if necessary. With C, embroider the eyes and nose in satin stitch (see page 152).

EARS

Turn under one corner of each ear and stitch to the centre of the ear, at the lower edge. Sew the ears in place, near the back of the head, stitching all around the lower edges.

LEGS

Flatten the tops of the legs and sew in place, stitching all around the tops of the thighs.

TAIL

Flatten the tail and, using the length of yarn left after fastening off, sew together the three stitches from each side of the last round to form a straight seam. Sew the tail in place. Weave in all ends.

Labrador

THIS LABRADOR, MADE IN EITHER GOLDEN OR CHOCOLATE, IS WORKED MAINLY IN DOUBLE CROCHET APART FROM THE TAIL, WHICH IS SHAPED USING HALF TREBLE STITCHES. IF YOU'RE MAKING A BLACK LABRADOR, USE BROWN YARN TO EMBROIDER THE FEATURES.

Materials

- Stylecraft Life DK, 75% premium acrylic, 25% wool (326yd/298m per 100g ball), or any DK yarn: 1 x 100g ball in 2446 Caramel or 2448 Bark (A)
- Approximately 20in (51cm) length of brown or black DK yarn, such as 2448 Bark or 2307 Black (B)
- 3.25mm (UK10:USD/3) crochet hook
- Blunt-ended yarn needle
- Toy stuffing

Size

- Approximately 9½in (24cm) body length from tip of nose to back of hind legs
- Approximately 8¼in (21cm) tall from top of head

Tension

22 sts and 24 rows to 4in (10cm) over double crochet using 3.25mm hook and yarn A. Use larger or smaller hook if necessary to obtain correct tension.

Method

The Labrador's body and legs are worked in continuous rounds of double crochet. The muzzle, head and neck are worked in one piece. The muzzle is crocheted in rounds and the top of the head is worked in rows. The neck is commenced by crocheting into unworked stitches at the underside of the muzzle and then along the edges of the rows of the top of the head. The neck is continued in rounds. The ears and tail are worked in rows. Double crochet and half treble stitches are used to shape the tail. The long edges of the tail are sewn together and a small amount of stuffing is inserted before sewing it in place. The toes on the paws are produced by crocheting bobbles. These appear on the reverse side of the fabric, so the work is turned before continuing with the leg. The eyes and nose are embroidered with yarn in satin stitch.

1 ch at beg of the row/round does not count as a st throughout.

Head

Starting at front of muzzle, with 3.25mm hook and A, make a magic loop (see page 145).

Round 1: 1 ch, 5 dc into loop (5 sts).

Round 2 (inc): (Dc2inc) 5 times (10 sts). Pull tightly on short end of yarn to close loop.

Round 3: (Dc2inc, 1 dc) 5 times (15 sts).

Round 4: 1 dc in each dc.

Round 5 (inc): (Dc2inc, 4 dc) 3 times (18 sts).

Round 6: 1 dc in each dc.

Round 7 (inc): (Dc2inc, 5 dc) 3 times (21 sts).

Round 8: 1 dc in each dc.

Round 9 (inc): (Dc2inc, 6 dc) 3 times (24 sts).

Rounds 10–11: 1 dc in each dc.

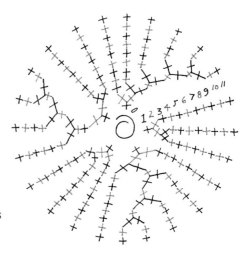

HEAD
ROUNDS 1–11

TOP OF HEAD

Row 1 (RS): 1 dc in next 18 dc, turn. Continue on these 18 sts.

Row 2 (WS) (inc): 1 ch, 1 dc in next dc, (dc2inc, 2 dc) 5 times, dc2inc, 1 dc in next dc, turn (24 sts).

Rows 3–5: 1 ch, 1 dc in each dc, turn.

Row 6 (dec): (Dc2tog, 4 dc) 4 times, turn (20 sts). Place a marker in the centre of this row.

Row 7 (dec): (Dc2tog, 3 dc) 4 times, turn (16 sts).

Row 8 (dec): (Dc2tog, 2 dc) 4 times, turn (12 sts).

Row 9 (dec): (Dc2tog, 1 dc) 4 times, turn (8 sts).

Row 10 (dec): (Dc2tog) 4 times (4 sts).

Break yarn and thread through last 4 stitches. Pull tightly on end of yarn. Fasten off.

KEY

- ⟳ MAGIC LOOP
- ⟋ CHAIN (CH)
- • SLIP STITCH (SL ST)
- ╂ DOUBLE CROCHET (DC)

- ⤬⤬ DC2INC
- ⤬⤬ DC2TOG
- ⊤ HALF TREBLE (HTR)
- ⊕ MAKE BOBBLE (MB)

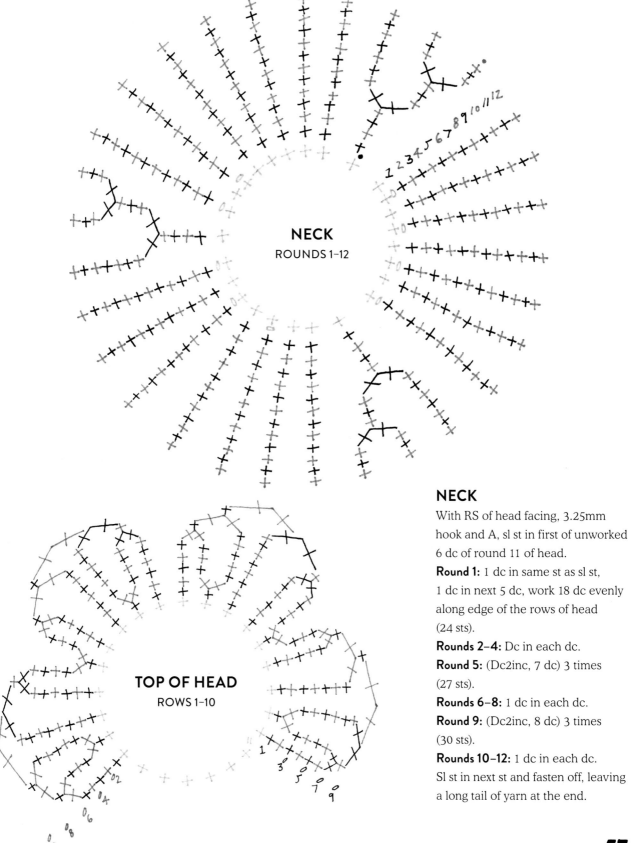

NECK
ROUNDS 1–12

TOP OF HEAD
ROWS 1–10

NECK

With RS of head facing, 3.25mm hook and A, sl st in first of unworked 6 dc of round 11 of head.

Round 1: 1 dc in same st as sl st, 1 dc in next 5 dc, work 18 dc evenly along edge of the rows of head (24 sts).

Rounds 2–4: Dc in each dc.

Round 5: (Dc2inc, 7 dc) 3 times (27 sts).

Rounds 6–8: 1 dc in each dc.

Round 9: (Dc2inc, 8 dc) 3 times (30 sts).

Rounds 10–12: 1 dc in each dc. Sl st in next st and fasten off, leaving a long tail of yarn at the end.

Ears (make 2)

With 3.25mm hook and A,
make 2 ch.
Row 1 (inc): 3 dc in 2nd ch from
hook, turn (3 sts).
Row 2: 1 ch, 1 dc in each dc, turn.
Rows 3–9 (inc): 1 ch, dc2inc,
1 dc in each dc to last st, turn (10 sts).
Rows 10–12: 1 ch, 1 dc in each dc,
turn.
Fasten off, leaving a long tail of yarn
at the end.

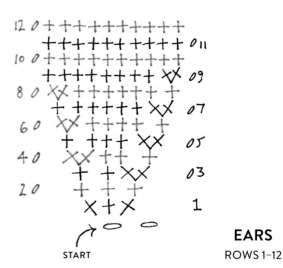

EARS
ROWS 1–12

Body

Starting at front of body, with
3.25mm hook and A, make 10 ch.
Round 1: 1 dc in 2nd ch from hook,
1 dc in next 7 ch, 2 dc in end ch,
1 dc in reverse side of next 8 ch.
Place a marker on the first stitch to
mark the top of the front of the body
(18 sts).
Round 2 (inc): (Dc2inc, 2 dc) 6 times
(24 sts).
Round 3 (inc): (Dc2inc, 3 dc) 6 times
(30 sts).
Round 4 (inc): (Dc2inc, 4 dc)
6 times (36 sts).
Round 5 (inc): (Dc2inc, 5 dc) 6 times
(42 sts).
Rounds 6–20: 1 dc in each dc.

BODY
ROUNDS 1–20

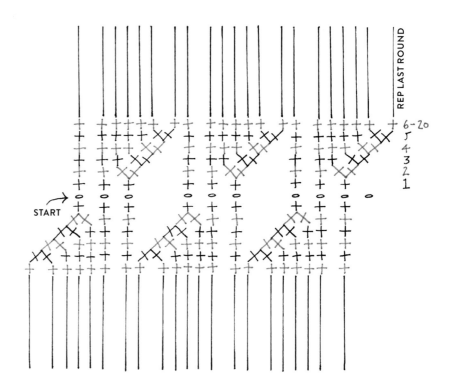

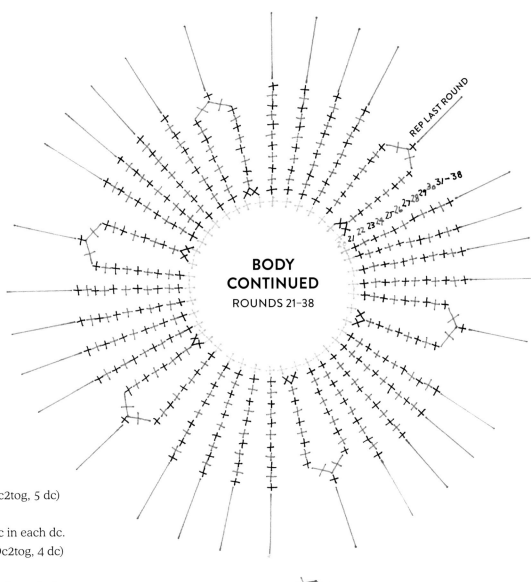

BODY
CONTINUED
ROUNDS 21–38

REP LAST ROUND

21 22 23 24 25 26 27 28 29 30 31–38

Round 21 (dec): (Dc2tog, 5 dc)
6 times (36 sts).

Rounds 22–29: 1 dc in each dc.

Round 30 (dec): (Dc2tog, 4 dc)
6 times (30 sts).

Rounds 31–38: 1 dc in each dc.
Stuff body before continuing.

Round 39 (dec): (Dc2tog, 3 dc)
6 times (24 sts).

Round 40 (dec): (Dc2tog, 2 dc)
6 times (18 sts).

Round 41 (dec): (Dc2tog, 1 dc)
6 times (12 sts).

Round 42 (dec): (Dc2tog) 6 times
(6 sts).

Break yarn and thread through last
6 stitches. Pull tightly on end of yarn
to close. Fasten off.

BODY
CONTINUED
ROUNDS 39–42

38 39 40 41 42

Front legs (make 2)

The bobbles appear on the reverse side of the work. This will be the right side. See page 148 for the instructions to make bobble (mb). Starting at the base of the paw, with 3.25mm hook and A, make a magic loop.

Round 1 (WS): 1 ch, 6 dc into loop (6 sts).

Round 2 (inc): (Dc2inc) 6 times (12 sts). Pull tightly on short end of yarn to close loop.

Round 3 (inc): (Dc2inc, 1 dc) 6 times (18 sts).

Round 4: 1 dc in next 10 dc, (mb, 1 dc in next dc) 4 times, turn.

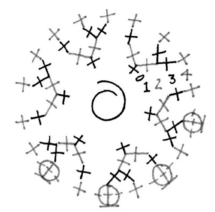

FRONT LEGS
ROUNDS 1–4

Round 5 (RS) (dec): 1 ch, 1 dc in first dc, (1 dc in next st, dc2tog) twice, 1 dc in next 11 dc (16 sts).

Round 6 (dec): (1 dc in next dc, dc2tog) twice, 1 dc in next 10 dc (14 sts).

Round 7 (dec): (Dc2tog, 1 dc in next dc) twice, 1 dc in next 8 dc (12 sts).

Rounds 8–17: 1 dc in each dc.

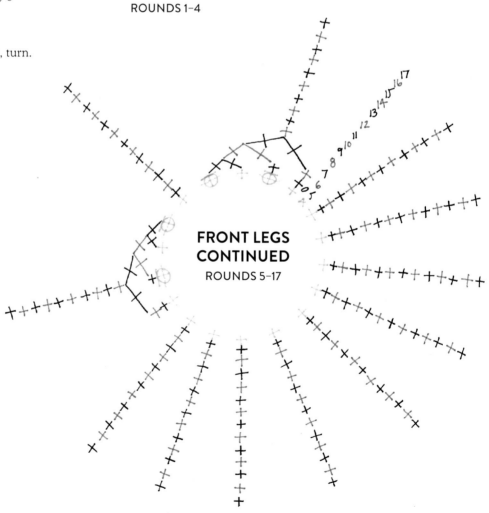

FRONT LEGS CONTINUED
ROUNDS 5–17

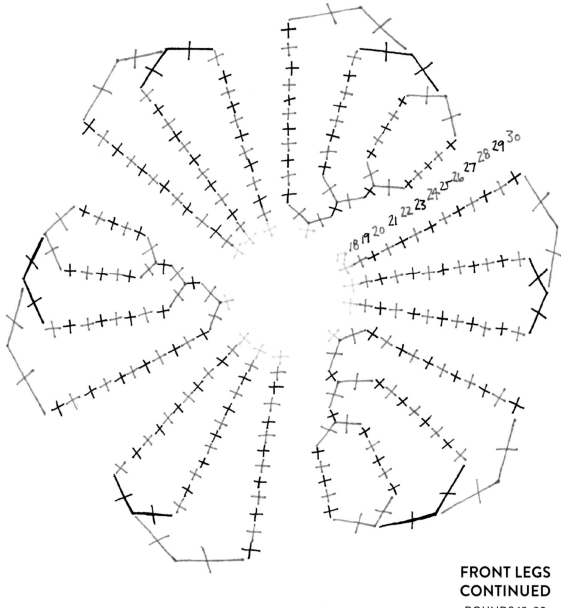

**FRONT LEGS
CONTINUED**
ROUNDS 18–30

Round 18 (inc): (Dc2inc, 3 dc)
3 times (15 sts).
Round 19: 1 dc in each dc.
Round 20 (inc): (Dc2inc, 4 dc)
3 times (18 sts).
Rounds 21: 1 dc in each dc.
Round 22 (inc): (Dc2inc, 5 dc)
3 times (21 sts).
Rounds 23–27: 1 dc in each dc.
Stuff leg before continuing.

Round 28 (dec): (Dc2tog, 5 dc)
3 times (18 sts).
Round 29 (dec): (Dc2tog, 1 dc)
6 times (12 sts).
Round 30 (dec): (Dc2tog) 6 times
(6 sts).
Break yarn and thread through last
round of stitches. Pull tightly on end
of yarn to close. Fasten off, leaving a
long tail of yarn at the end.

Hind legs (make 2)

Starting at the base of the paw, with 3.25mm hook and A, make a magic loop.

Rounds 1–15: Work as for rounds 1–15 of front legs.

SHAPE BACK OF LEG

Round 16: 1 dc in next 2 dc, ending at the side of the leg; 6 ch, skip the 6 dc at the front of the leg, 1 dc in next 4 dc.

Round 17: 1 dc in next 2 dc, 1 dc in next 6 ch, 1 dc in next 4 dc. Break yarn and thread through last round of stitches. Pull tightly on end of yarn to close and fasten off.

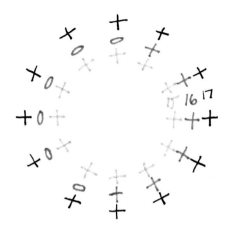

HIND LEGS
SHAPE BACK OF LEG
ROUNDS 16–17

SHAPE THIGH

With RS of leg facing, 3.25mm hook and A, sl st in first of skipped 6 dc.

Round 1: 1 dc in same st as sl st, 1 dc in next 5 dc, 1 dc in reverse side of next 6 ch (12 sts).

Round 2 (inc): (Dc2inc) 6 times, 1 dc in next 6 dc (18 sts).

Rounds 3–6: 1 dc in each dc.

Round 7 (inc): (Dc2inc, 2 dc) 6 times (24 sts).

Rounds 8–11: 1 dc in each dc.

Round 12 (inc): (Dc2inc, 3 dc) 6 times (30 sts).

Rounds 13–16: 1 dc in each dc.

Round 17 (dec): (Dc2tog, 3 dc) 6 times (24 sts).

Round 18 (dec): (Dc2tog, 2 dc) 6 times (18 sts).

Stuff leg before continuing.

Round 19 (dec): (Dc2tog, 1 dc) 6 times (12 sts).

Round 20 (dec): (Dc2tog) 6 times (6 sts).

Break yarn and thread through last round of stitches. Pull tightly on end of yarn to close. Fasten off, leaving a long tail of yarn at the end.

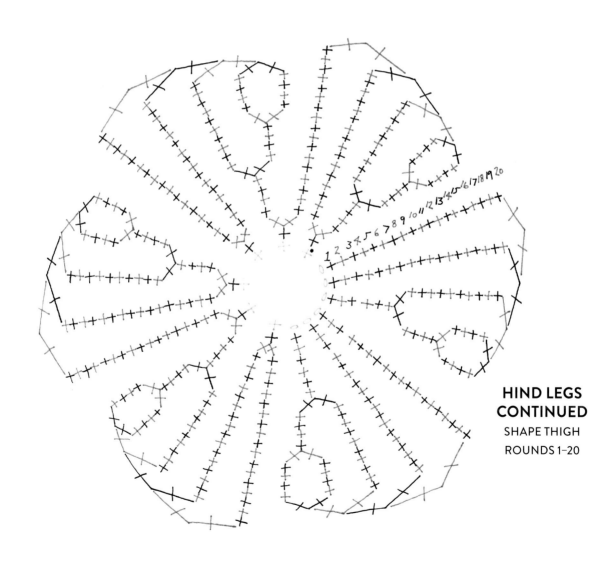

HIND LEGS CONTINUED

SHAPE THIGH

ROUNDS 1–20

Tail

With 3.25mm hook and A, make 20 ch.

Row 1: 1 dc in 2nd ch from hook, 1 dc in next 17 ch, 3 dc in end ch, 1 dc in reverse side of next 18 ch, turn (39 sts).

Row 2 (inc): 2 ch (does not count as a st), 1 htr in next 14 dc, 1 dc in next 5 dc, 3 dc in next dc, 1 dc in next 5 dc, 1 htr in next 14 dc, turn (41 sts).

Row 3 (dec): 1 ch, 1 dc in next 2 sts, (1 dc, dc2tog) 4 times, 1 dc in next 6 dc, 3 dc in next dc, 1 dc in next 6 dc, (dc2tog, 1 dc) 4 times, 1 dc in next 2 sts (35 sts).

Fasten off, leaving a long tail of yarn at the end.

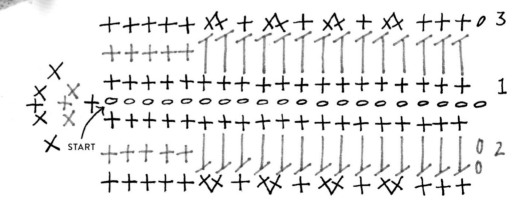

TAIL
ROWS 1–3

Making up

HEAD

Stuff the head. With the tail of yarn left after fastening off, sew the head in place, indicated by the marker at the top of the body. Stitch all around the neck edges and insert more stuffing into the neck if necessary. With yarn B, embroider the eyes and nose in satin stitch (see page 152).

EARS

Turn under the three stitches of the last row at the corner of an ear and sew the edges together. Align the edge of the ear with the row of stitches of the head, indicated by the marker, placing the folded corner at the top, face down. Repeat for the other ear, turning under the opposite corner. With the tips of the ears pointing towards the nose, sew the ears in place along the stitches of the last row. Dampen down the ears. Move the tip of each ear back towards the neck. Stick a pin through the tips and then into the neck to hold the ears in position. Remove the pins when the ears are dry.

LEGS

Flatten the tops of the legs and sew in place, stitching all around the tops of the thighs.

TAIL

Using the length of yarn left after fastening off, fold the tail lengthways and sew the long edges together with whip stitch (see page 151). Use the end of the crochet hook to push a small amount of stuffing into the tail. Sew the tail in place. Weave in the short ends of yarn.

Chihuahua

THIS CHIHUAHUA HAS A ROUND, APPLE-SHAPED HEAD.
ITS LARGE EARS ARE FORMED BY JOINING TWO PIECES TOGETHER
TO MAKE A FIRMER FABRIC SO THEY STAND UPRIGHT.

Materials

- Patons Wool DK, 100% virgin wool (137yd/125m per 50g ball), or any DK yarn:
  2 x 50g balls in 00105 Camel (A)
- Approximately 20in (51cm) length of black DK yarn, such as 00199 Black (B)
- 3.25mm (UK10:USD/3) crochet hook
- Blunt-ended yarn needle
- Toy stuffing

Size

- Approximately 6¼in (16cm) body length from tip of nose to back of hind legs
- Approximately 7¼in (18.5cm) tall from top of head (excluding ears)

Tension

22 sts and 26 rows to 4in (10cm) over double crochet using 3.25mm hook and yarn A. Use larger or smaller hook if necessary to obtain correct tension.

Method

The Chihuahua's head, body and legs are worked in continuous rounds of double crochet. The muzzle, head and neck are worked in one piece. The ears and tail are worked in rows. Each ear is made up of two crocheted pieces that are joined by crocheting into each stitch of both pieces at the same time. The curve in the tail is formed by decreasing in the last row. The long edges of the tail are sewn together and a small amount of stuffing is inserted before sewing it in place. The toes on the paws are produced by crocheting bobbles. These appear on the reverse side of the fabric, so the work is turned before continuing with the leg. The eyes and nose are embroidered with yarn in satin stitch.

1 ch at beg of the row/round does not count as a st throughout.

Head

Starting at front of muzzle, with 3.25mm hook and A, make a magic loop (see page 145).

Round 1: 1 ch, 6 dc into loop (6 sts).

Round 2 (inc): (Dc2inc) 6 times (12 sts). Pull tightly on short end of yarn to close loop.

Rounds 3–5: 1 dc in each dc.

Round 6 (inc): (Dc2inc) 6 times, 1 dc in next 6 dc (18 sts).

Round 7 (inc): 1 dc in next 3 dc, (dc2inc) 6 times, 1 dc in next 9 dc (24 sts).

Round 8 (inc): 1 dc in next 4 dc, (dc2inc, 1 dc) 6 times, 1 dc in next 2 dc, finishing 6 sts before the end of the round (30 sts).

HEAD
ROUNDS 1–8
DIVIDE FOR NECK
ROUNDS 9–10
TOP OF HEAD
ROUNDS 11–20

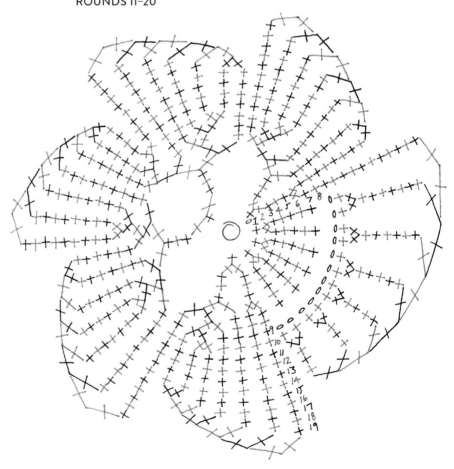

KEY

- ⟳ MAGIC LOOP
- ⟋ CHAIN (CH)
- • SLIP STITCH (SL ST)
- ✛ DOUBLE CROCHET (DC)
- ✕✕ DC2INC
- ✕✕ DC2TOG
- ⊕ MAKE BOBBLE (MB)

DIVIDE FOR NECK

Round 9: Make 12 ch, skip next 6 dc, 1 dc in next 4 dc, (dc2inc, 2 dc) 6 times, 1 dc in next 2 dc (12 ch and 30 dc).

Round 10 (inc): 1 dc in next 12 ch, 1 dc in next 4 dc, *(dc2inc, 3 dc) 3 times, 1 dc in next dc; rep from * once more (48 sts).

TOP OF HEAD

Round 11 (dec): (Dc2tog) 6 times, 1 dc in next 36 dc (42 sts).

Rounds 12–14: 1 dc in each dc.

Round 15 (dec): (Dc2tog, 5 dc) 6 times (36 sts).

Round 16 (dec): (Dc2tog, 4 dc) 6 times (30 sts).

Round 17 (dec): (Dc2tog, 3 dc) 6 times (24 sts).

Round 18 (dec): (Dc2tog, 2 dc) 6 times (18 sts).

Round 19 (dec): (Dc2tog, 1 dc) 6 times (12 sts).

Round 20 (dec): (Dc2tog) 6 times (6 sts).

Break yarn and thread through last round of stitches. Pull tightly on end of yarn to close. Fasten off.

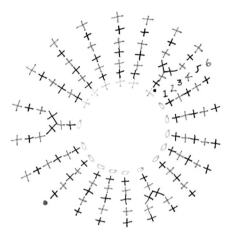

NECK
ROUNDS 1–6

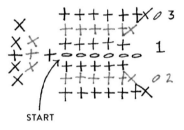

EARS
ROWS 1–3

JOIN EAR PIECES
INSERT HOOK INTO EACH STITCH OF BOTH EAR PIECES AT SAME TIME TO JOIN

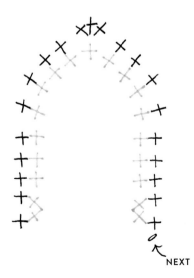

NEXT

NECK

With RS of head facing, 3.25mm hook and A, sl st in first of skipped 6 dc.

Round 1: 1 dc in same st as sl st, 1 dc in next 5 dc, 1 dc in reverse side of next 12 ch (18 sts).

Round 2: 1 dc in each dc.

Round 3: (Dc2inc, 5 dc) 3 times (21 sts).

Rounds 4–5: 1 dc in each dc.

Round 6: 1 dc in next 10 dc, ending at the side of the neck. Sl st in next st and fasten off, leaving a long tail of yarn at the end.

Ears (make 2)

With 3.25mm hook and A, make 6 ch.

Row 1: 1 dc in 2nd ch from hook, 1 dc in next 3 ch, 3 dc in next ch, 1 dc in reverse side of next 4 ch, turn (11 sts).

Row 2 (inc): 1 ch, dc2inc, 1 dc in next 4 dc, 3 dc in next dc, 1 dc in next 4 dc, dc2inc, turn (15 sts).

Row 3 (inc): 1 ch, dc2inc, 1 dc in next 6 dc, 3 dc in next dc, 1 dc in next 6 dc, dc2inc (19 sts). Fasten off. Make one more piece to match the first. Turn work at the end and do not fasten off.

JOIN EAR PIECES

Place the two ear pieces together.

Next: 1 ch, inserting the hook under both loops of each stitch of both pieces at the same time to join, 1 dc in next 9 dc, 3 dc in next dc, 1 dc in next 9 dc (21 sts). Fasten off, leaving a long length of yarn at the end.

Body

Starting at front of body, with
3.25mm hook and A, make 10 ch.
Round 1: 1 dc in 2nd ch from hook,
1 dc in next 7 ch, 2 dc in end
ch, 1 dc in reverse side of next 8 ch.
Place a marker on the first stitch
to mark the top of the front of the
body (18 sts).
Round 2 (inc): (Dc2inc, 2 dc)
6 times (24 sts).
Round 3 (inc): (Dc2inc, 3 dc)
6 times (30 sts).
Round 4 (inc): (Dc2inc, 4 dc)
6 times (36 sts).
Rounds 5–15: 1 dc in each dc.
Round 16 (dec): (Dc2tog, 4 dc)
6 times (30 sts).
Rounds 17–23: 1 dc in each dc.

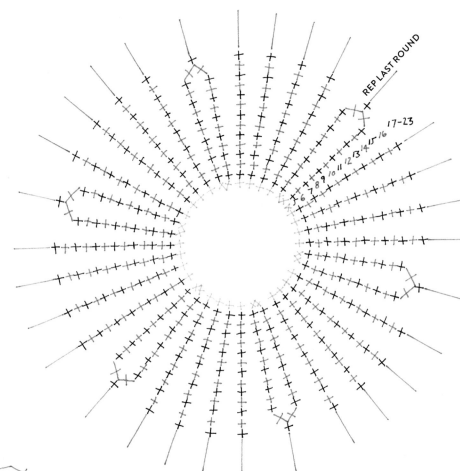

BODY CONTINUED
ROUNDS 24–34

BODY
FOR ROUNDS 1–4,
FOLLOW CHART FOR BODY
OF LABRADOR (SEE PAGE 58)
ROUNDS 5–23

Round 24 (dec): (Dc2tog, 3 dc)
6 times (24 sts).
Rounds 25–31: 1 dc in each dc.
Stuff body before continuing.
Round 32 (dec): (Dc2tog, 2 dc)
6 times (18 sts).
Round 33 (dec): (Dc2tog, 1 dc)
6 times (12 sts).
Round 34 (dec): (Dc2tog) 6 times
(6 sts).
Break yarn and thread through last
6 stitches. Pull tightly on end of yarn
to close. Fasten off.

Front legs (make 2)

The bobbles appear on the reverse side of the work. This will be the right side. See page 148 for instructions to make bobble (mb). Starting at the base of the paw, with 3.25mm hook and A, make a magic loop.

Round 1 (WS): 1 ch, 6 dc into loop (6 sts).

Round 2 (inc): (Dc2inc) 6 times (12 sts). Pull tightly on short end of yarn to close loop.

Round 3 (inc): 1 dc in next 7 dc, (dc2inc, 1 dc) twice, 1 dc in next dc (14 sts).

Round 4: 1 dc in next 6 dc, (mb, 1 dc in next dc) 4 times, turn.

Round 5 (RS) (dec): 1 ch, 1 dc in first dc, (1 dc in next st, dc2tog) twice, 1 dc in next 7 dc (12 sts).

Round 6 (dec): (1 dc in next dc, dc2tog) twice, 1 dc in next 6 dc (10 sts).

Rounds 7–17: 1 dc in each dc.

Round 18 (inc): (Dc2inc, 4 dc) twice (12 sts).

Round 19: 1 dc in each dc.

Round 20 (inc): (Dc2inc, 3 dc) 3 times (15 sts).

Rounds 21–23: 1 dc in each dc. Stuff leg before continuing.

Round 24 (dec): (Dc2tog, 1 dc) 5 times (10 sts).

Round 25 (dec): (Dc2tog) 5 times (5 sts).

Break yarn and thread through last round of stitches. Pull tightly on end of yarn to close. Fasten off, leaving a long tail of yarn at the end.

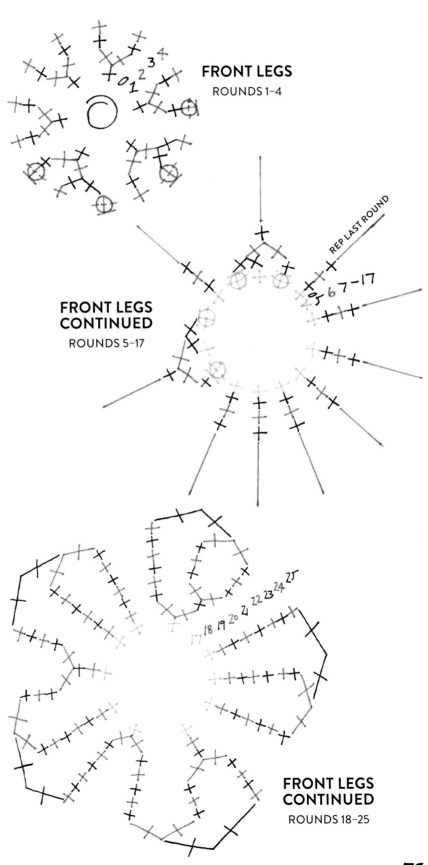

FRONT LEGS
ROUNDS 1–4

FRONT LEGS CONTINUED
ROUNDS 5–17

FRONT LEGS CONTINUED
ROUNDS 18–25

Hind legs (make 2)

Starting at the base of the paw, with 3.25mm hook and A, make a magic loop.

Rounds 1–12: Work as for rounds 1–12 of front legs.

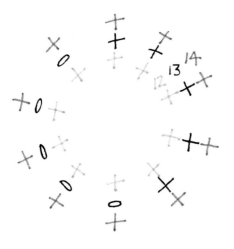

HIND LEGS
SHAPE BACK OF LEG
ROUNDS 13–14

SHAPE BACK OF LEG

Round 13: 1 dc in next 2 dc, ending at the side of the leg; 5 ch, skip the 5 dc at the front of the leg, 1 dc in next 3 dc.

Round 14: 1 dc in next 2 dc, 1 dc in next 5 ch, 1 dc in next 3 dc. Break yarn and thread through last round of stitches. Pull tightly on end of yarn to close and fasten off.

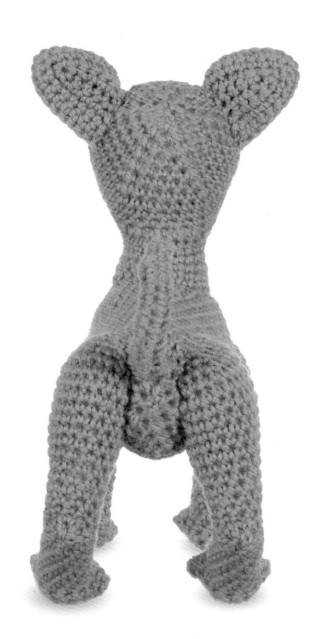

SHAPE THIGH

With RS of leg facing, 3.25mm hook and A, sl st in first of skipped 5 dc.

Round 1: 1 dc in same st as sl st, 1 dc in next 4 dc, 1 dc in reverse side of next 5 ch (10 sts).

Rounds 2–5: 1 dc in each dc.

Round 6 (inc): (Dc2inc, 1 dc) 5 times (15 sts).

Round 7: 1 dc in each dc.

Round 8 (inc): (Dc2inc, 4 dc) 3 times (18 sts).

Round 9: 1 dc in each dc.

HIND LEGS CONTINUED
SHAPE THIGH
ROUNDS 1–9

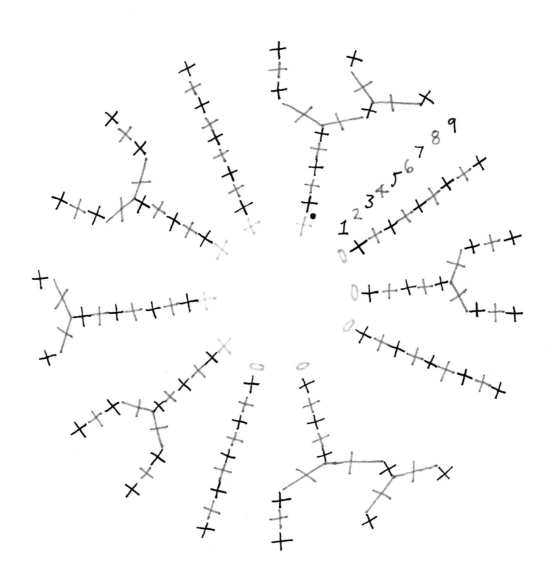

Round 10 (inc): (Dc2inc, 5 dc)
3 times (21 sts).

Round 11: 1 dc in each dc.

Round 12 (inc): (Dc2inc, 6 dc)
3 times (24 sts).

Rounds 13–14: 1 dc in each dc.
Stuff leg before continuing.

Round 15 (dec): (Dc2tog, 2 dc)
6 times (18 sts).

Round 16 (dec): (Dc2tog, 1 dc)
6 times (12 sts).

Round 17 (dec): (Dc2tog) 6 times
(6 sts).

Break yarn and thread through last
round of stitches. Pull tightly on end
of yarn to close. Fasten off, leaving a
long tail of yarn at the end.

**HIND LEGS
CONTINUED**

SHAPE THIGH
ROUNDS 10–17

Tail

With 3.25mm hook and A, make 18 ch.

Row 1: 1 dc in 2nd ch from hook, 1 dc in next 15 ch, 3 dc in end ch, 1 dc in reverse side of next 16 ch, turn (35 sts).

Row 2 (dec): 1 ch, 1 dc in next 2 sts, (1 dc, dc2tog) 4 times, 1 dc in next 3 dc, 3 dc in next dc, 1 dc in next 3 dc, (dc2tog, 1 dc) 4 times, 1 dc in next 2 sts (29 sts).

Fasten off, leaving a long tail of yarn at the end.

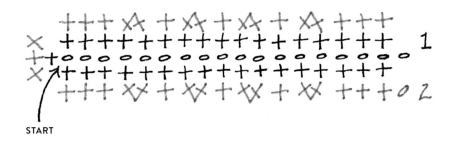

TAIL
ROWS 1–2

Making up

HEAD

Stuff the head. With the tail of yarn left after fastening off, sew the head in place, indicated by the marker at the top of the body. Stitch all around the neck edges and insert more stuffing into the neck if necessary. With yarn B, embroider the eyes and nose in satin stitch (see page 152).

EARS

Turn under one corner of each ear and stitch to the centre of the ear, at the lower edge. Sew the ears in place, near the back of the head, stitching all around the lower edges.

LEGS

Flatten the tops of the legs and sew in position, stitching all around the tops of the thighs.

TAIL

Using the length of yarn left after fastening off, fold the tail lengthways and sew the long edges together with whip stitch (see page 151). Use the end of the crochet hook to push a small amount of stuffing into the tail. Sew the tail in place.

Weave in the short ends of yarn.

Dalmatian

THE SPOTS OF THE DALMATIAN ARE EMBROIDERED IN BLACK YARN AFTER SEWING THE CROCHETED PIECES TOGETHER, SO YOU CAN CHOOSE EXACTLY HOW MANY MARKINGS YOU HAVE AND WHERE YOU WANT THEM TO GO.

Materials

- King Cole Luxury Merino DK, 100% merino superwash (153yd/140m per 50g ball), or any DK yarn:
  2 x 50g balls in 2610 White (A)
  1 x 50g ball in 2611 Black (B)
- 3.5mm (UK9:USE/4) crochet hook
- Blunt-ended yarn needle
- Toy stuffing

Size

- Approximately 9⅞in (25cm) body length from tip of nose to back of hind legs
- Approximately 8⅞in (22.5cm) tall from top of head

Tension

22 sts and 26 rows to 4in (10cm) over double crochet using 3.5mm hook and yarn A. Use larger or smaller hook if necessary to obtain correct tension.

Method

The Dalmatian's body and legs are worked in continuous rounds of double crochet. The muzzle, head and neck are worked in one piece. The muzzle is crocheted in rounds and the top of the head is worked in rows. The neck is commenced by crocheting into unworked stitches at the underside of the muzzle and then along the edges of the rows that make up the top of the head. The neck is continued in rounds. The ears and tail are worked in rows. The stitches are decreased in the last row to form a curve in the tail. The long edges of the tail are sewn together and a small amount of stuffing is inserted before sewing it in place. The toes on the paws are produced by crocheting bobbles. These appear on the reverse side of the fabric, so the work is turned before continuing with the leg. The eyes, nose and spots are embroidered with yarn in satin stitch.

1 ch at beg of the row/round does not count as a st throughout.

Head

Starting at front of muzzle, with 3.5mm hook and A, make a magic loop (see page 145).

Round 1: 1 ch, 5 dc into loop (5 sts).

Round 2 (inc): (Dc2inc) 5 times (10 sts). Pull tightly on short end of yarn to close loop.

Round 3: (Dc2inc, 1 dc) 5 times (15 sts).

Rounds 4–5: 1 dc in each dc.

Round 6 (inc): (Dc2inc, 4 dc) 3 times (18 sts).

Rounds 7–8: 1 dc in each dc.

Round 9 (inc): (Dc2inc, 5 dc) 3 times (21 sts).

Rounds 10–12: 1 dc in each dc.

HEAD
ROUNDS 1–12

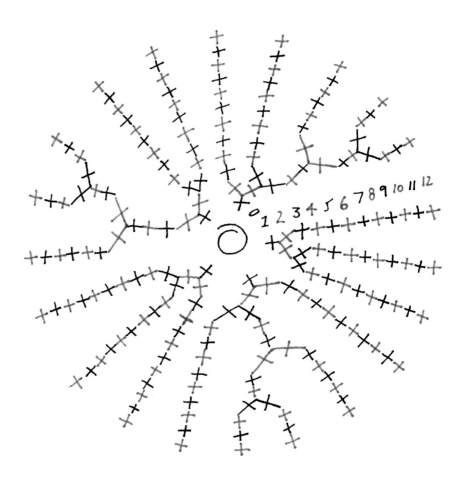

TOP OF HEAD

Row 1 (RS): 1 dc in next 16 dc, turn. Continue on these 16 sts.

Row 2 (WS) (inc): 1 ch, (dc2inc, 1 dc) 8 times, turn (24 sts).

Rows 3–6: 1 ch, 1 dc in each dc, turn. Place a marker in the centre of row 5.

Row 7 (dec): (Dc2tog, 2 dc) 6 times, turn (18 sts).

Row 8 (dec): (Dc2tog, 1 dc) 6 times, turn (12 sts).

Row 9 (dec): (Dc2tog) 6 times (6 sts). Break yarn and thread through last 6 stitches. Pull tightly on end of yarn. Fasten off.

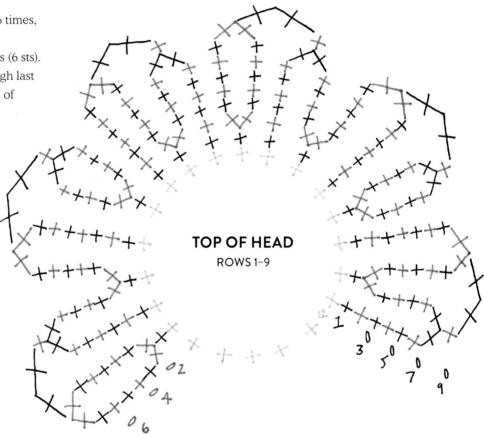

TOP OF HEAD
ROWS 1–9

KEY

- ⟳ MAGIC LOOP
- ⬮ CHAIN (CH)
- • SLIP STITCH (SL ST)
- ┼ DOUBLE CROCHET (DC)
- ✕ DC2INC
- ✕ DC2TOG
- ⊕ MAKE BOBBLE (MB)

NECK

With RS of head facing, 3.5mm hook and A, sl st in first of unworked 5 dc of round 12 of head.

Round 1: 1 dc in same st as sl st, 1 dc in next 4 dc, work 16 dc evenly along edge of the rows of head (21 sts).

Rounds 2–6: Dc in each dc.
Round 7: (Dc2inc, 6 dc) 3 times (24 sts).
Rounds 8–12: 1 dc in each dc. Sl st in next st and fasten off, leaving a long tail of yarn at the end.

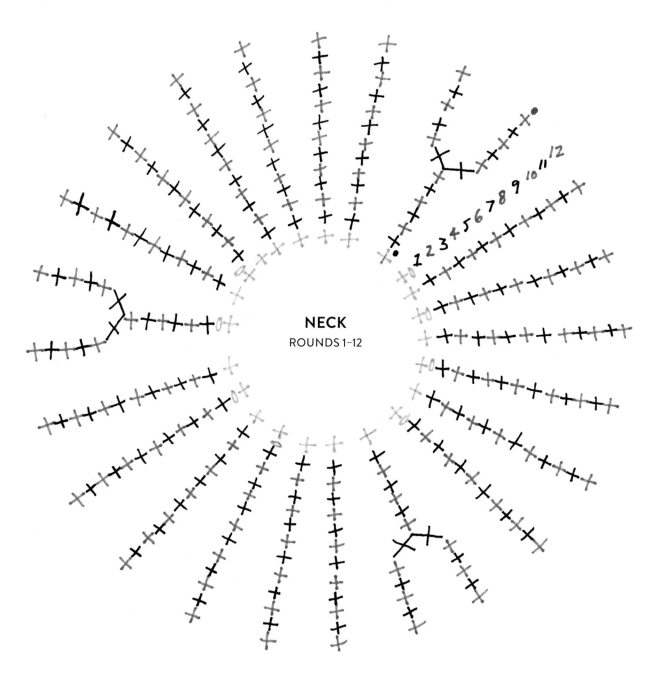

NECK
ROUNDS 1–12

Ears (make 2)

With 3.5mm hook and B,
make 2 ch.
Row 1 (inc): 3 dc in 2nd ch from
hook, turn (3 sts).
Row 2: 1 ch, 1 dc in each dc, turn.
Rows 3–9 (inc): 1 ch, dc2inc, 1 dc in
each dc to last st, turn (10 sts).
Row 10: 1 ch, 1 dc in each dc, turn.
Fasten off, leaving a long tail of yarn
at the end.

EARS
ROWS 1–10

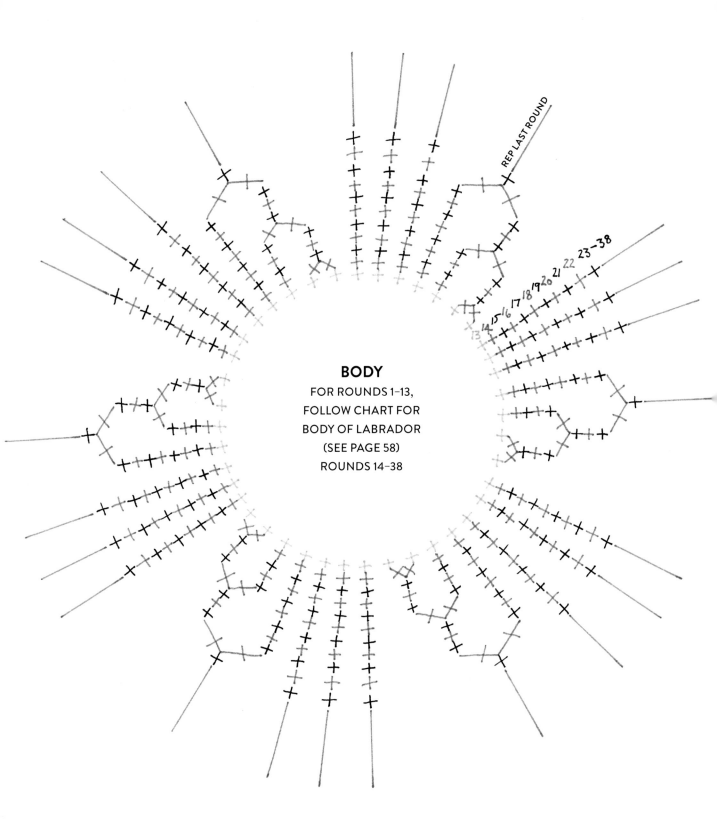

BODY
FOR ROUNDS 1–13,
FOLLOW CHART FOR
BODY OF LABRADOR
(SEE PAGE 58)
ROUNDS 14–38

REP LAST ROUND

13 14 15 16 17 18 19 20 21 22 23–38

Body

Starting at front of body, with 3.5mm hook and A, make 10 ch.

Round 1: 1 dc in 2nd ch from hook, 1 dc in next 7 ch, 2 dc in end ch, 1 dc in reverse side of next 8 ch. Place a marker on the first stitch to mark the top of the front of the body (18 sts).

Round 2 (inc): (Dc2inc, 2 dc) 6 times (24 sts).

Round 3 (inc): (Dc2inc, 3 dc) 6 times (30 sts).

Round 4 (inc): (Dc2inc, 4 dc) 6 times (36 sts).

Round 5 (inc): (Dc2inc, 5 dc) 6 times (42 sts).

Rounds 6–13: 1 dc in each dc.

Round 14 (dec): (Dc2tog, 5 dc) 6 times (36 sts).

Rounds 15–17: 1 dc in each dc.

Round 18 (dec): (Dc2tog, 4 dc) 6 times (30 sts).

Rounds 19–21: 1 dc in each dc.

Round 22 (dec): (Dc2tog, 3 dc) 6 times (24 sts).

Rounds 23–38: 1 dc in each dc. Stuff body before continuing.

Round 39 (dec): (Dc2tog, 2 dc) 6 times (18 sts).

Round 40 (dec): (Dc2tog, 1 dc) 6 times (12 sts).

Round 41 (dec): (Dc2tog) 6 times (6 sts).

Break yarn and thread through last 6 stitches. Pull tightly on end of yarn to close. Fasten off.

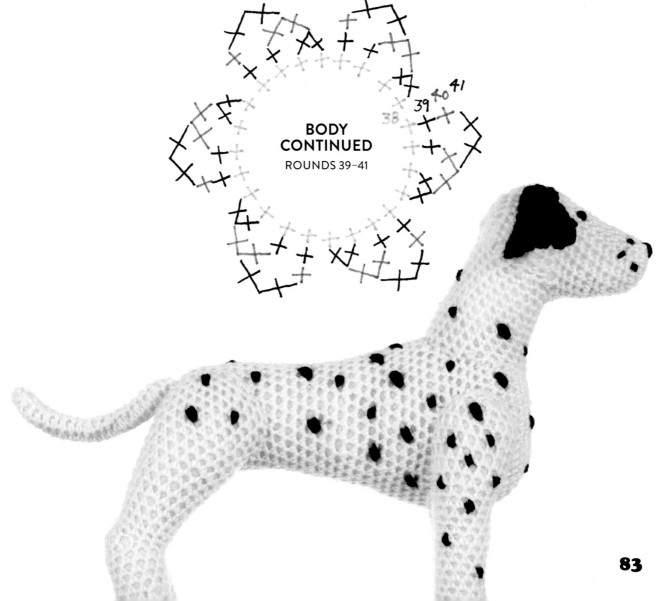

BODY CONTINUED
ROUNDS 39–41

83

Front legs (make 2)

The bobbles appear on the reverse side of the work. This will be the right side. See page 148 for the instructions to make bobble (mb). Starting at the base of the paw, with 3.5mm hook and A, make a magic loop.

Round 1 (WS): 1 ch, 6 dc into loop (6 sts).

Round 2 (inc): (Dc2inc) 6 times (12 sts). Pull tightly on short end of yarn to close loop.

Round 3 (inc): (Dc2inc, 2 dc) 4 times (16 sts).

Round 4: 1 dc in next 8 dc, (mb, 1 dc in next dc) 4 times, turn.

Round 5 (RS) (dec): 1 ch, 1 dc in first dc, (1 dc in next st, dc2tog) twice, 1 dc in next 9 dc (14 sts).

Round 6 (dec): (1 dc in next dc, dc2tog) twice, 1 dc in next 8 dc (12 sts).

Rounds 7–19: 1 dc in each dc.

Round 20 (inc): (Dc2inc, 3 dc) 3 times (15 sts).

Round 21–22: 1 dc in each dc.

Round 23 (inc): (Dc2inc, 4 dc) 3 times (18 sts).

Rounds 24–28: 1 dc in each dc. Stuff leg before continuing.

Round 29 (dec): (Dc2tog, 1 dc) 6 times (12 sts).

Round 30 (dec): (Dc2tog) 6 times (6 sts).

Break yarn and thread through last round of stitches. Pull tightly on end of yarn to close. Fasten off, leaving a long tail of yarn at the end.

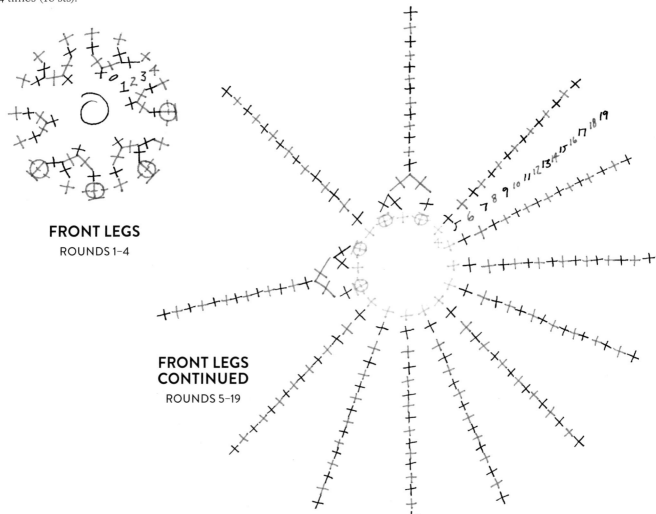

FRONT LEGS
ROUNDS 1–4

FRONT LEGS CONTINUED
ROUNDS 5–19

FRONT LEGS CONTINUED

ROUNDS 20–30

Hind legs (make 2)

Starting at the base of the paw, with 3.5mm hook and A, make a magic loop.

Rounds 1–15: Work as for rounds 1–15 of front legs.

SHAPE BACK OF LEG

Round 16: 1 dc in next 3 dc, ending at the side of the leg; 6 ch, skip the 6 dc at the front of the leg, 1 dc in next 3 dc.

Round 17: 1 dc in next 3 dc, 1 dc in next 6 ch, 1 dc in next 3 dc. Break yarn and thread through last round of stitches. Pull tightly on end of yarn to close and fasten off.

HIND LEGS
SHAPE BACK OF LEG
ROUNDS 16–17

SHAPE THIGH

With RS of leg facing, 3.5mm hook and A, sl st in first of skipped 6 dc.

Round 1: 1 dc in same st as sl st, 1 dc in next 5 dc, 1 dc in reverse side of next 6 ch (12 sts).

Round 2 (inc): (Dc2inc, 1 dc) 3 times, 1 dc in next 6 dc (15 sts).

Rounds 3–5: 1 dc in each dc.

Round 6 (inc): (Dc2inc, 4 dc) 3 times (18 sts).

Rounds 7–9: 1 dc in each dc.

Round 10 (inc): (Dc2inc, 5 dc) 3 times (21 sts).

Rounds 11–13: 1 dc in each dc.

Round 14 (inc): (Dc2inc, 6 dc) 3 times (24 sts).

Rounds 15–17: 1 dc in each dc. Stuff leg before continuing.

Round 18 (dec): (Dc2tog, 2 dc) 6 times (18 sts).

Round 19 (dec): (Dc2tog, 1 dc) 6 times (12 sts).

Round 20 (dec): (Dc2tog) 6 times (6 sts).

Break yarn and thread through last round of stitches. Pull tightly on end of yarn to close. Fasten off, leaving a long tail of yarn at the end.

HIND LEGS CONTINUED
SHAPE THIGH
ROUNDS 1–20

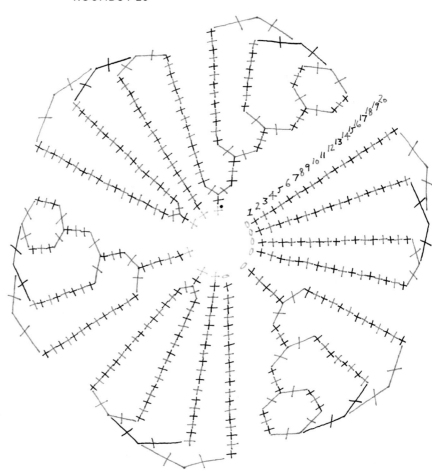

Tail

With 3.5mm hook and A,
make 23 ch.
Row 1: 1 dc in 2nd ch from hook,
1 dc in next 20 ch, 3 dc in end ch,
1 dc in reverse side of next 21 ch,
turn (45 sts).
Row 2 (dec): 1 ch, 1 dc in next 2 sts,
(1 dc, dc2tog) 4 times, 1 dc in next
8 dc, 3 dc in next dc, 1 dc in next
8 dc, (dc2tog, 1 dc) 4 times, 1 dc in
next 2 sts (39 sts).
Fasten off, leaving a long tail of yarn
at the end.

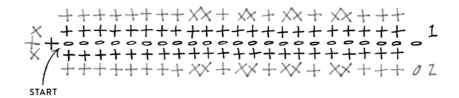

TAIL
ROWS 1–2

START

Making up

HEAD
Stuff the head. With the tail of yarn
left after fastening off, sew the head
in place, indicated by the marker at
the top of the body. Stitch all
around the neck edges and insert
more stuffing into the neck, if
necessary. With yarn B, embroider
the eyes and nose in satin stitch
(see page 152).

EARS
Turn under three stitches of the last
row at the corner of an ear and sew
the edges together. Align the edge
of the ear with the row of stitches of
the head, indicated by the marker,
placing the folded corner at the top,
face down. Repeat for the other ear,
turning under the opposite corner.
With the tips of the ears pointing
towards the nose, sew the ears in
place along the stitches of the last
row. Dampen down the ears. Move
the tip of each ear back towards the
neck. Stick a pin through the tips
and then into the neck to hold the
ears in position. Remove the pins
when the ears are dry.

LEGS
Flatten the tops of the legs and sew
in place, stitching all around the
tops of the thighs.

TAIL
Using the length of yarn left after
fastening off, fold the tail lengthways
and sew the long edges together
with whip stitch (see page 151). Use
the end of the crochet hook to push
a small amount of stuffing into the
tail. Sew the tail in place.

SPOTS
Embroider different size spots,
where desired, in satin stitch with
yarn B. Work two stitches close
together for the small spots around
the nose and three to four stitches for
the larger spots on the body and legs.
Weave in the short ends of yarn.

Spaniel

THIS SPANIEL'S BLACK FACIAL FEATURES ARE CROCHETED WITH
ADDITIONAL MARKINGS EMBROIDERED ON THE FACE AND LEGS. TO MAKE
A BLUE ROAN SPANIEL, SIMPLY OMIT THE TAN EMBROIDERY.

Materials

- King Cole Vogue DK, 100% cotton (113yd/103m per 50g ball), or any DK yarn:
  2 x 50g balls in 2111 Cool Grey (A)
- King Cole Panache DK, 50% wool, 50% premium acrylic (342yd/312m per 100g ball), or any DK yarn:
  1 x 100g ball in 2070 Charcoal (B)
- Approximately 12in (30cm) length of brown DK yarn, such as 2064 Chestnut (C) for the eyes
- Approximately 47¼in (120cm) length of tan or orange DK yarn, such as 2075 Ginger (D) for the markings above the eyes and muzzle
- 3.25mm (UK10:USD/3) crochet hook
- Blunt-ended yarn needle
- Toy stuffing

Size

- Approximately 9in (23cm) body length from tip of nose to back of hind legs
- Approximately 7¼in (18.5cm) tall from top of head

Tension

22 sts and 24 rows to 4in (10cm) over double crochet using 3.25mm hook and yarn A. Use larger or smaller hook if necessary to obtain correct tension.

Method

The Spaniel's body, legs and ears are worked in continuous rounds of double crochet. The muzzle, head and neck are worked in one piece. The muzzle is crocheted in rounds, and the face and top of the head are worked in rows. The black markings on the face are crocheted, carrying the unused yarn across the work. The neck is commenced by crocheting into unworked stitches at the underside of the muzzle and then along the edges of the rows that make up the top of the head. The neck is continued in rounds. Loop stitch is used to produce the feathered coat on the body and legs. It is also used on the long ears. The tail is worked in rows. Double crochet, half treble and slip stitches form the tapered shape. The long edges of the tail are sewn together and a small amount of stuffing is inserted before sewing it in place. The toes on the paws are produced by crocheting bobbles. The bobbles on the paws and the loop stitches appear on the reverse side of the fabric. The eyes, nose and other markings are embroidered to finish the dog.

1 ch at beg of the row/round does not count as a st throughout.

Head

Starting at front of muzzle, with 3.25mm hook and A, make a magic loop (see page 145).
Round 1: 1 ch, 5 dc into loop (5 sts).
Round 2 (inc): (Dc2inc) 5 times (10 sts). Pull tightly on short end of yarn to close loop.
Round 3: (Dc2inc, 1 dc) 5 times (15 sts).
Rounds 4–5: 1 dc in each dc.
Round 6 (inc): (Dc2inc, 4 dc) 3 times (18 sts).
Round 7: 1 dc in each dc, turn.

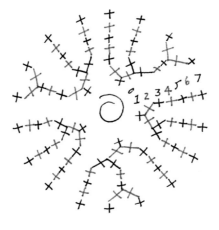

HEAD
ROUNDS 1–7

FACE

The following is worked in rows. Carry unused yarn across the WS of the work (see page 149).
Row 1 (WS): 1 ch, 1 dc in next 3 dc. Join B in last dc; with B, work 1 dc in next 4 dc; with A, work 1 dc in next 4 dc; with B, work 1 dc in next 4 dc; with A, work 1 dc in next 3 dc, sl st in first dc, turn.
Row 2 (RS): 1 dc in next 3 dc; with B, 1 dc in next 5 dc; with A, work 1 dc in next 2 dc; with B, work 1 dc in next 5 dc, with A, work 1 dc in next 3 dc, turn.
Row 3 (inc): 1 ch, 1 dc in next 3 dc, with B, work (dc2inc, 1 dc) twice, dc2inc; with A, work 1 dc in next 2 dc; with B, (dc2inc, 1 dc) twice, dc2inc, turn, finishing 3 sts before the end (24 sts).

KEY

⊙ MAGIC LOOP

⊘ CHAIN (CH)

• SLIP STITCH (SL ST)

╋ DOUBLE CROCHET (DC)

XX DC2INC

XX DC2TOG

┳ HALF TREBLE (HTR)

⚇ LOOP STITCH (LP ST)

⊕ MAKE BOBBLE (MB)

TOP OF HEAD

Row 4: With B, work 1 ch, 1 dc in next 8 dc; with A, work 1 dc in next 2 dc; with B, work 1 dc in next 8 dc, turn.

Continue on these 18 dc.

Row 5: With B, work 1 ch, 1 dc in next dc, (dc2inc, 2 dc) twice, dc2inc; with A, work 1 dc in next 2 dc; with B, (dc2inc, 2 dc) twice, dc2inc, 1 dc in next dc, turn (24 sts).

Row 6: With B, work 1 ch, 1 dc in next 11 dc; with A, work 1 dc in next 2 dc; with B, work 1 dc in next 11 dc, turn.

Rows 7–8: With B, work 1 ch, 1 dc in next 10 dc; with A, work 1 dc in next 4 dc; with B, work 1 dc in next 10 dc, turn.

Row 9 (dec): With B, work 1 ch, (dc2tog, 2 dc) twice, dc2tog; with A, work 1 dc in next 4 dc; with B, (dc2tog, 2 dc) twice, dc2tog, turn (18 sts).

Continue with A.

Row 10 (dec): 1 ch, (dc2tog, 1 dc) 6 times, turn (12 sts).

Row 11 (dec): 1 ch, (dc2tog) 6 times (6 sts).

Break yarn and thread through last 6 stitches. Pull tightly on end of yarn. Fasten off.

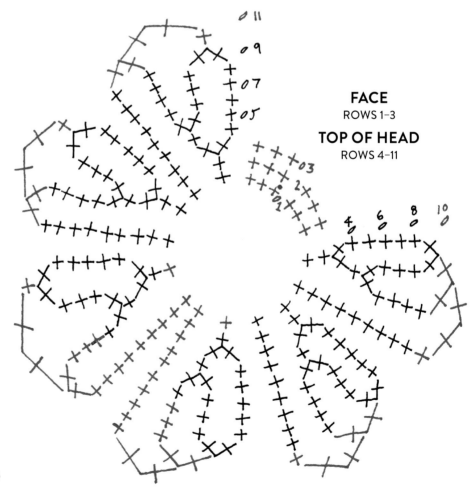

FACE
ROWS 1–3

TOP OF HEAD
ROWS 4–11

COLOUR KEY

FOR FACE AND TOP OF HEAD

NECK

With RS of head facing, 3.25mm hook and A, sl st in first of 6 unworked dc of round 3 of face.

Round 1: 1 dc in same st as sl st, 1 dc in next 5 dc, work 14 dc evenly along edge of the rows of head (20 sts).

Rounds 2–7: Dc in each dc.

Round 8: 1 dc in next 12 dc, (dc2inc, 1 dc) 4 times (24 sts).

Rounds 9–10: 1 dc in each dc. Sl st in next st and fasten off, leaving a long tail of yarn at the end.

NECK
ROUNDS 1–10

Ears (make 2)

The loops appear on the reverse side of the work. This will be the right side. See page 148 for instructions on loop stitch (lp st). With 3.25mm hook and A, make 10 ch.

Round 1: 1 dc in 2nd ch from hook, 1 dc in next 7 ch, 2 dc in end ch, 1 dc in reverse side of next 8 ch (18 sts).

Round 2: 1 lp st in each dc.

Round 3 (inc): (Dc2inc, 2 dc) 6 times (24 sts).

Rounds 4–5: 1 dc in each dc.

Round 6: 1 lp st in each dc.

Rounds 7–8: 1 dc in each dc.

Round 9 (dec): (Dc2tog, 2 dc) 6 times (18 sts).

Round 10: 1 lp st in each dc.

Rounds 11–12: 1 dc in each dc. Turn ear right side out. Continue crocheting as before, inserting the hook into each stitch from the WS.

Round 13 (dec): (Dc2tog, 1 dc) 6 times (12 sts).

Round 14: 1 lp st in each dc.

Round 15 (dec): (Dc2tog) 6 times (6 sts). Fasten off, leaving a long tail of yarn at the end.

EARS
ROUNDS 1–2

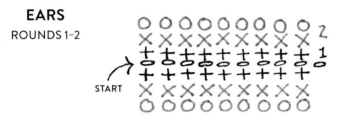

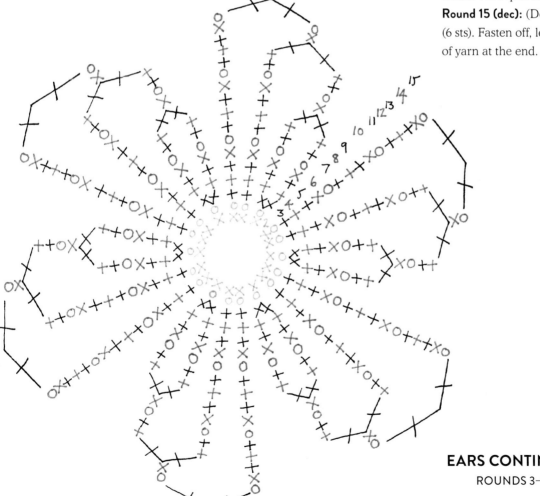

EARS CONTINUED
ROUNDS 3–15

Body

The loops appear on the reverse side of the work. This will be the right side.

Starting at front of body, with 3.25mm hook and A, make 13 ch.

Round 1: 1 dc in 2nd ch from hook, 1 dc in next 10 ch, 2 dc in end ch, 1 dc in reverse side of next 11 ch. Place a marker on the first stitch to mark the top of the front of the body (24 sts).

Round 2: 1 lp st in each dc.

Round 3 (inc): (Dc2inc, 3 dc) 6 times (30 sts).

Round 4 (inc): (Dc2inc, 4 dc) 6 times (36 sts).

Round 5 (inc): (Dc2inc, 5 dc) 6 times (42 sts).

Round 6: 1 lp st in each dc.

Rounds 7–9: 1 dc in each dc.

Round 10: Rep round 6.

Rounds 11–17: 1 dc in each dc.

Round 18 (dec): (Dc2tog, 5 dc) 6 times (36 sts).

Rounds 19–25: 1 dc in each dc.

Turn body right side out. Continue crocheting as before, inserting the hook into each stitch from the WS.

BODY
ROUNDS 1–9

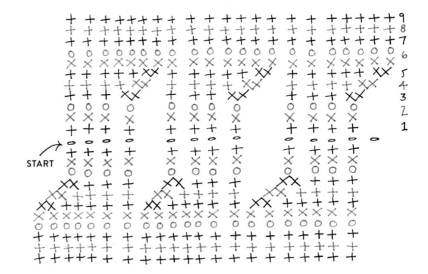

BODY CONTINUED
ROUNDS 10–25

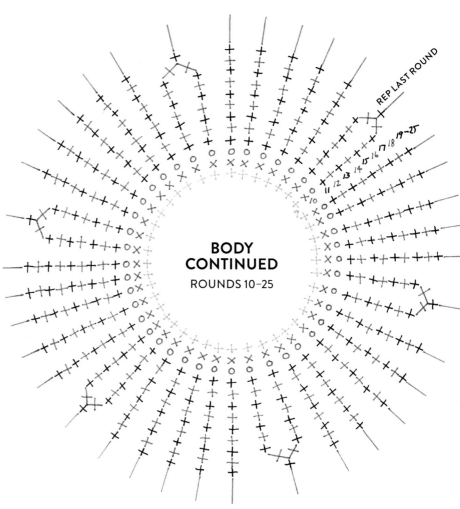

Round 26 (dec): (Dc2tog, 4 dc) 6 times (30 sts).

Rounds 27–35: 1 dc in each dc. Stuff body before continuing.

Round 36 (dec): (Dc2tog, 3 dc) 6 times (24 sts).

Round 37 (dec): (Dc2tog, 2 dc) 6 times (18 sts).

Round 38 (dec): (Dc2tog, 1 dc) 6 times (12 sts).

Round 39 (dec): (Dc2tog) 6 times (6 sts).

Break yarn and thread through last 6 stitches. Pull tightly on end of yarn to close. Fasten off.

BODY CONTINUED
ROUNDS 26–39

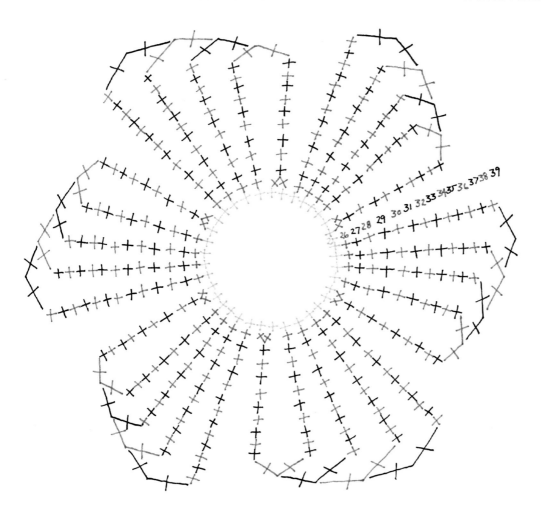

Front legs (make 2)

The bobbles and loops appear on the reverse side of the work. This will be the right side. See page 148 for instructions to make bobble (mb). Starting at the base of the paw, with 3.25mm hook and A, make a magic loop.

Round 1: 1 ch, 6 dc into loop (6 sts).

Round 2 (inc): (Dc2inc) 6 times (12 sts). Pull tightly on short end of yarn to close loop.

Round 3 (inc): (Dc2inc, 2 dc) 4 times (16 sts).

Round 4: 1 dc in next 8 dc, (mb, 1 dc in next dc) 4 times.

Round 5 (dec): 1 dc in next 9 dc, (dc2tog, 1 dc) twice, 1 dc in next dc (14 sts).

Round 6 (dec): 1 dc in next 8 dc, (dc2tog, 1 dc) twice (12 sts).

Rounds 7–9: 1 dc in each dc.

Round 10: 1 dc in next 3 dc, 1 lp st in next 6 dc, 1 dc in next 3 dc.

Rounds 11–13: 1 dc in each dc.

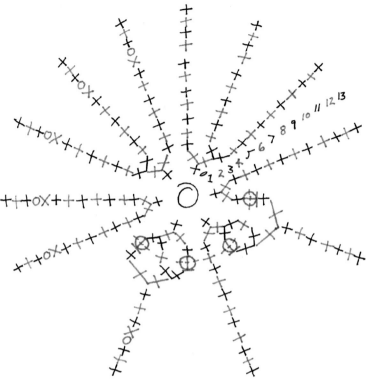

FRONT LEGS
ROUNDS 1–13

**FRONT LEGS
CONTINUED**
ROUNDS 14–23

Round 14: 1 dc in next 4 dc, 1 lp st in next 6 dc, 1 dc in next 2 dc.

Rounds 15–17: 1 dc in each dc.

Round 18 (inc): (Dc2inc, 3 dc) 3 times (15 sts).

Round 19: 1 dc in each dc.

Round 20 (inc): (Dc2inc, 4 dc) 3 times (18 sts).

Round 21: 1 dc in each dc.
Turn leg right side out. Stuff leg before continuing.
Continue crocheting as before, inserting the hook into each stitch from the WS.

Round 22 (dec): (Dc2tog, 1 dc) 6 times (12 sts).

Round 23 (dec): (Dc2tog) 6 times (6 sts).
Break yarn and thread through last round of stitches. Pull tightly on end of yarn to close. Fasten off, leaving a long tail of yarn at the end.

Hind legs (make 2)

Starting at the base of the paw, with 3.25mm hook and A, make a magic loop.

Rounds 1–9: Work as for rounds 1–9 of front legs.

Round 10: 1 lp st in next 3 dc, 1 dc in next 6 dc, 1 lp st in next 3 dc.

Round 11: 1 dc in next 9 dc, ending at the side of the leg.

SHAPE BACK OF LEG

Round 12: Make 6 ch, skip the 6 dc at the front of the leg, 1 dc in next 6 dc.

Round 13: 1 dc in next 6 ch, 1 dc in next 6 dc.

Break yarn and thread through last round of stitches. Pull tightly on end of yarn to close and fasten off.

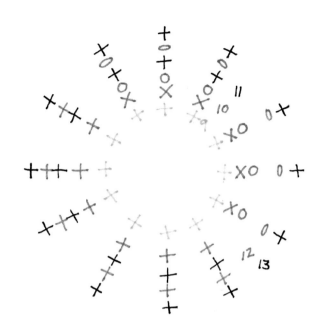

HIND LEGS
ROUNDS 10–11
SHAPE BACK OF LEG
ROUNDS 12–13

SHAPE THIGH

With WS of leg facing, 3.5mm hook and A, sl st in first of skipped 6 dc.

Round 1: 1 dc in same st as sl st, 1 dc in next 5 dc, 1 dc in reverse side of next 6 ch (12 sts).

Round 2 (inc): (Dc2inc) 6 times, 1 dc in next 6 dc (18 sts).

Round 3: 1 lp st in next 12 dc, 1 dc in next 6 dc.

Rounds 4–5: 1 dc in each dc.

Round 6 (inc): (Dc2inc, 2 dc) 6 times (24 sts).

Round 7: 1 dc in next 4 dc, lp st in next 12 dc, 1 dc in next 8 dc.

Rounds 8–10: 1 dc in each dc.

Round 11: 1 dc in next 5 dc, lp st in next 12 dc, 1 dc in next 7 dc.

Rounds 12–13: 1 dc in each dc.

Turn leg right side out. Stuff leg before continuing.

Continue crocheting as before, inserting the hook into each stitch from the WS.

Round 14 (dec): (Dc2tog, 2 dc) 6 times (18 sts).

Round 15 (dec): (Dc2tog, 1 dc) 6 times (12 sts).

Round 16 (dec): (Dc2tog) 6 times (6 sts).

Break yarn and thread through last round of stitches. Pull tightly on end of yarn to close. Fasten off, leaving a long tail of yarn at the end.

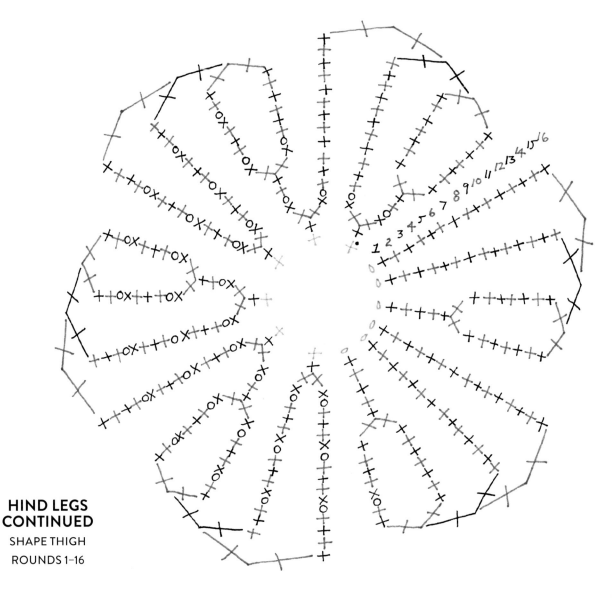

**HIND LEGS
CONTINUED**
SHAPE THIGH
ROUNDS 1–16

Tail

With 3.25mm hook and A,
make 8 ch.

Row 1: 1 dc in 2nd ch from hook,
1 dc in next 3 ch, 1 htr in next 3 ch,
turn (7 sts).

Row 2: 1 ch, 1 dc in each st, turn.

Row 3: 1 ch, 1 dc in next 4 dc, 1 htr
in next 3 dc, turn.

Row 4: 1 ch, 1 dc in next 4 sts, sl st
in next 3 dc.

Fasten off, leaving a long tail of yarn
at the end.

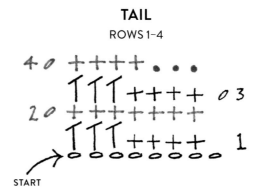

TAIL
ROWS 1–4

START

Making up

HEAD

Stuff the head. With the tail of yarn
left after fastening off, sew the head
in place, indicated by the marker at
the top of the body. Stitch all around
the neck edges. Tuck the loops that
will be covered by the head inside
the neck and take care not to catch
the loops that appear around the
outside edges of the neck in the
stitches. Insert more stuffing into
the neck if necessary. Embroider
the eyes in C, nose in B and the
markings above the eyes in D, in
satin stitch (see page 152). Following
the shape of the double crochet
stitches, embroider V-shaped stitches
(see page 152) over the front of the
muzzle in D, and use B for additional
markings up the centre of the
muzzle. Markings on the body and
legs can also be embroidered in B,
in satin stitch and straight stitches
(see page 152), as desired.

EARS

Flatten the ear and sew together the
three stitches from each side of the
last round to form a straight seam.
Sew an ear to each side of the head.

LEGS

Flatten the tops of the legs and sew
in place, stitching all around the
tops of the thighs.

TAIL

Using the length of yarn left after
fastening off, fold the tail lengthways
and sew the long edges together
with whip stitch (see page 151).
Use the end of the crochet hook to
push a small amount of stuffing into
the tail. Sew the tail in place. Weave
in the short ends of yarn.

Yorkshire Terrier

THE YORKSHIRE TERRIER'S LONG COAT IS FORMED BY ADDING TASSELS TO THE HEAD, NECK, BODY AND TOPS OF THE LEGS. THE STRANDS OF YARN ARE TRIMMED TO NEATEN AND CAN BE CUT TO ANY LENGTH DESIRED.

Materials

- King Cole Bamboo Cotton, 50% bamboo viscose, 50% cotton (252yd/230m per 100g ball), or any DK yarn:
  1 x 100g ball in 3330 Truffle (A)
  1 x 100g ball in 534 Black (B)
- 3.25mm (UK10:USD/3) crochet hook
- Blunt-ended yarn needle
- Toy stuffing

Size

- Approximately 7½in (19cm) body length from tip of nose to back of hind legs
- Approximately 6¾in (17cm) tall from top of head (excluding ears)

Tension

22 sts and 24 rows to 4in (10cm) over double crochet using 3.25mm hook and yarn A. Use larger or smaller hook if necessary to obtain correct tension.

Method

The Yorkshire Terrier's head, body and legs are worked in continuous rounds of double crochet. The muzzle, head and neck are worked in one piece. The ears and tail are crocheted in rows. Each ear is made up of two crocheted parts that are joined by crocheting into each stitch of both pieces at the same time. The long edges of the tail are sewn together and a small amount of stuffing is inserted before sewing it in place. The loop stitches on the tail are cut through. The toes on the paws are produced by crocheting bobbles. These appear on the reverse side of the fabric, so the work is turned before continuing with the leg. Lengths of yarn are attached to the posts of the stitches to form the long coat. The eyes and nose are embroidered with yarn in satin stitch.

1 ch at beg of the row/round does not count as a st throughout.

Head

Starting at front of muzzle, with 3.25mm hook and A, make a magic loop (see page 145).

Round 1: 1 ch, 6 dc into loop (6 sts).
Round 2 (inc): (Dc2inc) 6 times (12 sts). Pull tightly on short end of yarn to close loop.
Rounds 3–4: 1 dc in each dc.
Round 5 (inc): (Dc2inc, 3 dc) 3 times (15 sts).
Round 6: 1 dc in each dc.

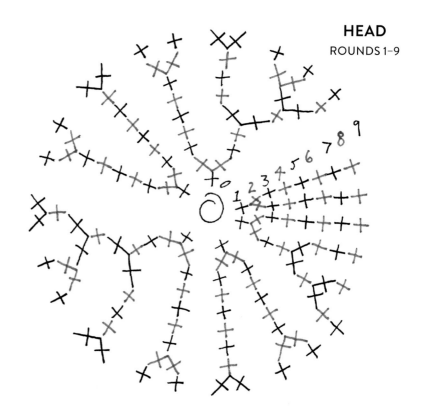

HEAD
ROUNDS 1–9

Round 7 (inc): (Dc2inc, 4 dc) 3 times (18 sts).
Round 8 (inc): 1 dc in next dc, (dc2inc, 1 dc) 6 times, 1 dc in next 5 dc (24 sts).
Round 9 (inc): 1 dc in next 3 dc, (dc2inc, 2 dc) 5 times, 1 dc in next dc, finishing 5 sts before the end, turn (29 sts).

TOP OF HEAD

Row 1 (WS): 1 ch, 1 dc in next 24 dc, turn.
Continue on these 24 sts.
Rows 2–5: 1 ch, 1 dc in each dc, turn. Place a marker in the centre of row 5.
Row 6 (WS) (dec): 1 ch, (dc2tog, 2 dc) 6 times, turn (18 sts).
Row 7 (dec): 1 ch, (dc2tog, 1 dc) 6 times, turn (12 sts).

Row 8 (dec): 1 ch, (dc2tog) 6 times (6 sts).
Break yarn and thread through last 6 stitches. Pull tightly on end of yarn. Fasten off.

NECK

With RS of head facing, 3.25mm hook and A, sl st in first of unworked 5 dc of round 9 of head.
Round 1: 1 dc in same st as sl st, 1 dc in next 4 dc, work 14 dc evenly along edge of the rows of head (19 sts).
Rounds 2–4: Dc in each dc.
Round 5: (Dc2inc, 1 dc) 4 times, 1 dc in next 11 dc (23 sts).
Round 6: Dc in each dc.
Round 7: 1 dc in next 13 dc. Sl st in next st and fasten off, leaving a long tail of yarn at the end.

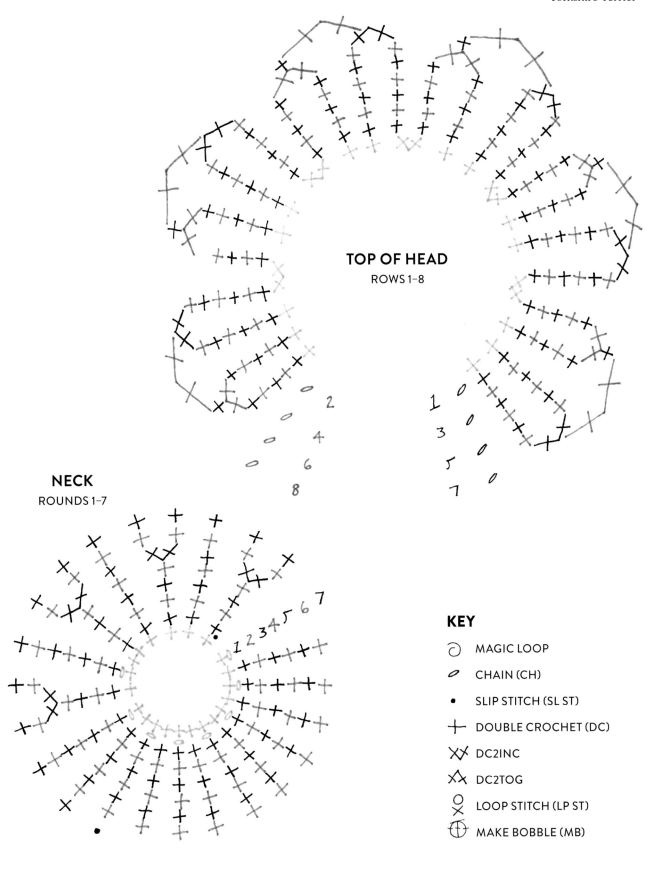

TOP OF HEAD
ROWS 1–8

NECK
ROUNDS 1–7

KEY

⟳ MAGIC LOOP

⬭ CHAIN (CH)

• SLIP STITCH (SL ST)

╋ DOUBLE CROCHET (DC)

⤬ DC2INC

⋀ DC2TOG

⨂ LOOP STITCH (LP ST)

⊕ MAKE BOBBLE (MB)

Ears (make 2)

With 3.25mm hook and A, make 5 ch.

Row 1: 1 dc in 2nd ch from hook, 1 dc in next 2 ch, 3 dc in next ch, 1 dc in reverse side of next 3 ch, turn (9 sts).

Row 2 (inc): 1 ch, dc2inc, 1 dc in next 3 dc, 3 dc in next dc, 1 dc in next 3 dc, dc2inc (13 sts). Fasten off. Make one more piece to match the first. Turn work at the end and do not fasten off.

JOIN EAR PIECES

Place the two ear pieces together.

Next: 1 ch, inserting the hook under both loops of each stitch of both pieces at the same time to join, 1 dc in next 6 dc, 3 dc in next dc, 1 dc in next 6 dc (15 sts). Fasten off, leaving a long length of yarn at the end.

EARS
ROWS 1–2

START

JOIN EAR PIECES
INSERT HOOK INTO EACH STITCH OF BOTH EAR PIECES AT SAME TIME TO JOIN

NEXT

Body

Starting at front of body, with 3.25mm hook and A, make 10 ch.

Round 1: 1 dc in 2nd ch from hook, 1 dc in next 7 ch, 2 dc in end ch, 1 dc in reverse side of next 8 ch. Place a marker on the first stitch to mark the top of the front of the body (18 sts).

Round 2 (inc): (Dc2inc, 2 dc) 6 times (24 sts).

Round 3 (inc): (Dc2inc, 3 dc) 6 times (30 sts).

Round 4 (inc): (Dc2inc, 4 dc) 6 times (36 sts).

Rounds 5–7: 1 dc in each dc. Join B in last dc. Continue with B.

Rounds 8–15: 1 dc in each dc.

Round 16 (dec): (Dc2tog, 4 dc) 6 times (30 sts).

Rounds 17–22: 1 dc in each dc.

Round 23 (dec): (Dc2tog, 3 dc) 6 times (24 sts).

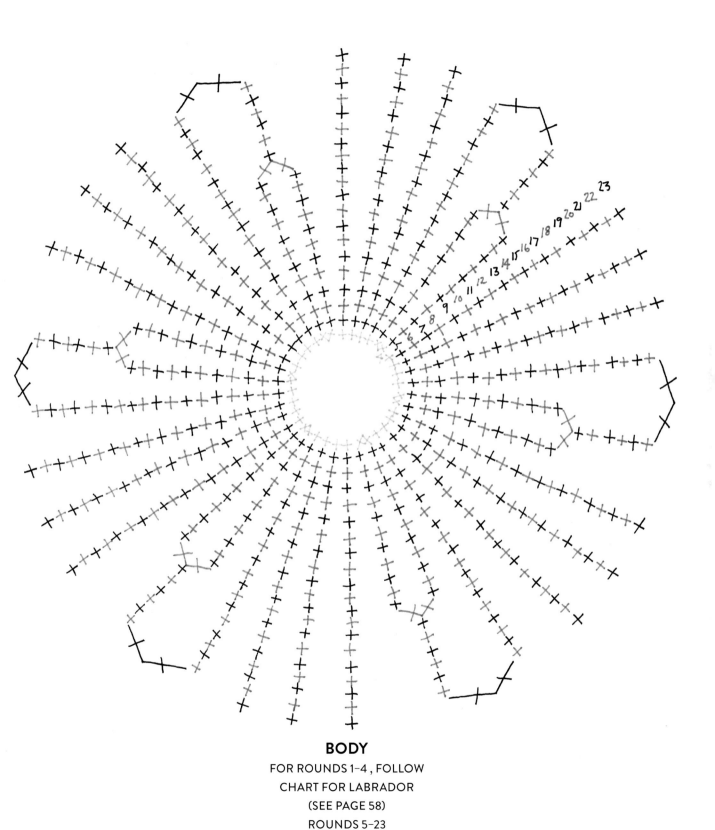

BODY
FOR ROUNDS 1-4 , FOLLOW
CHART FOR LABRADOR
(SEE PAGE 58)
ROUNDS 5-23

Rounds 24–31: 1 dc in each dc.
Stuff body before continuing.
Round 32 (dec): (Dc2tog, 2 dc)
6 times (18 sts).
Round 33 (dec): (Dc2tog, 1 dc)
6 times (12 sts).
Round 34 (dec): (Dc2tog) 6 times
(6 sts).
Break yarn and thread through last
6 stitches. Pull tightly on end of yarn
to close. Fasten off.

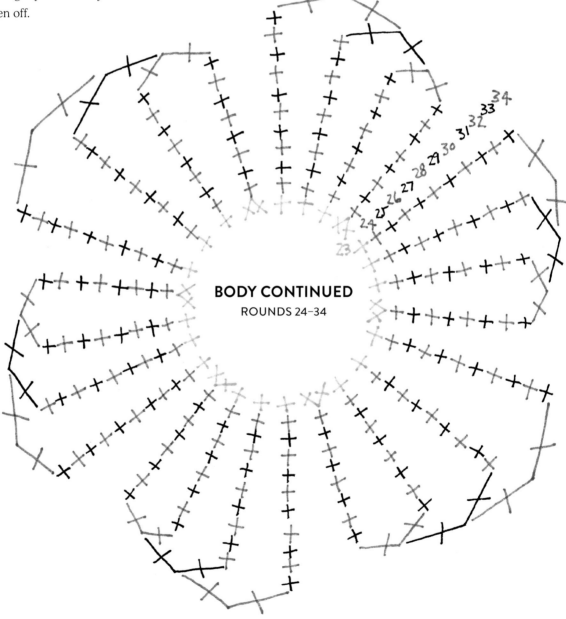

BODY CONTINUED
ROUNDS 24–34

Front legs (make 2)

The bobbles appear on the reverse side of the work. This will be the right side. See page 148 for instructions to make bobble (mb). Starting at the base of the paw, with 3.25mm hook and A, make a magic loop.

Round 1 (WS): 1 ch, 6 dc into loop (6 sts).

Round 2 (inc): (Dc2inc) 6 times (12 sts). Pull tightly on short end of yarn to close loop.

Round 3 (inc): (Dc2inc, 2 dc) 4 times (16 sts).

Round 4: 1 dc in next 8 dc, (mb, 1 dc in next dc) 4 times, turn.

Round 5 (RS) (dec): 1 ch, 1 dc in first dc, (1 dc in next st, dc2tog) twice, 1 dc in next 9 dc (14 sts).

Round 6 (dec): (1 dc in next dc, dc2tog) twice, 1 dc in next 8 dc (12 sts).

Rounds 7–17: 1 dc in each dc.

Round 18 (inc): (Dc2inc, 3 dc) 3 times (15 sts).

Rounds 19–23: 1 dc in each dc. Stuff leg before continuing.

Round 24 (dec): (Dc2tog, 1 dc) 5 times (10 sts).

Round 25 (dec): (Dc2tog) 5 times (5 sts).

Break yarn and thread through last round of stitches. Pull tightly on end of yarn to close. Fasten off, leaving a long tail of yarn at the end.

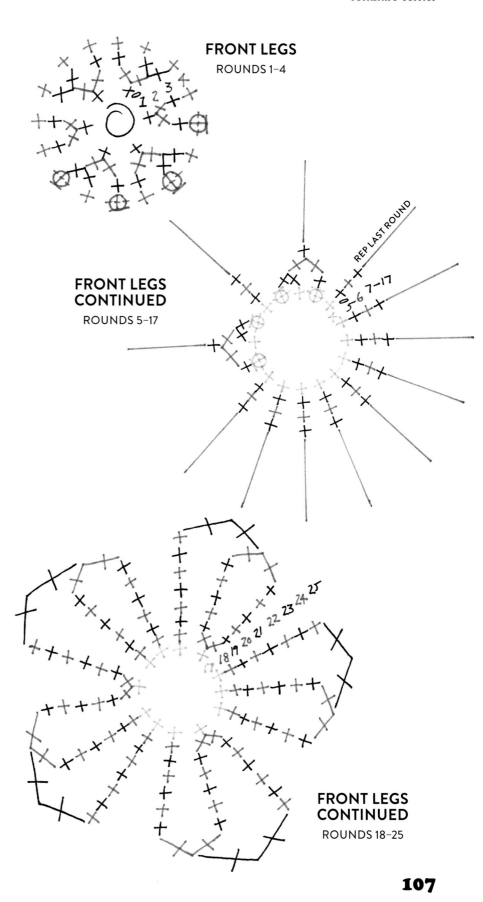

FRONT LEGS
ROUNDS 1–4

FRONT LEGS CONTINUED
ROUNDS 5–17

REP LAST ROUND

FRONT LEGS CONTINUED
ROUNDS 18–25

107

Hind legs (make 2)

Starting at the base of the paw, with 3.25mm hook and A, make a magic loop.

Rounds 1–12: Work as for rounds 1–12 of front legs.

SHAPE BACK OF LEG

Round 13: 1 dc in next dc, ending at the side of the leg; 6 ch, skip the 6 dc at the front of the leg, 1 dc in next 5 dc.

Round 14: 1 dc in next dc, 1 dc in next 6 ch, 1 dc in next 5 dc. Break yarn and thread through last round of stitches. Pull tightly on end of yarn to close and fasten off.

SHAPE THIGH

With RS of leg facing, 3.25mm hook and B, sl st in first of skipped 6 dc of round 13.

Round 1: 1 dc in same st as sl st, 1 dc in next 5 dc, 1 dc in reverse side of next 6 ch (12 sts).

Round 2: 1 dc in each dc.

Round 3 (inc): (Dc2inc, 3 dc) 3 times (15 sts).

Rounds 4–5: 1 dc in each dc.

Round 6 (inc): (Dc2inc, 4 dc) 3 times (18 sts).

Rounds 7–8: 1 dc in each dc.

Round 9 (inc): (Dc2inc, 5 dc) 3 times (21 sts).

Rounds 10–11: 1 dc in each dc.

Round 12 (inc): (Dc2inc, 6 dc) 3 times (24 sts).

Rounds 13–14: 1 dc in each dc. Stuff leg before continuing.

Round 15 (dec): (Dc2tog, 2 dc) 6 times (18 sts).

Round 16 (dec): (Dc2tog, 1 dc) 6 times (12 sts).

Round 17 (dec): (Dc2tog) 6 times (6 sts). Break yarn and thread through last round of stitches. Pull tightly on end of yarn to close. Fasten off, leaving a long tail of yarn at the end.

HIND LEGS

SHAPE BACK OF LEG

ROUNDS 13–14

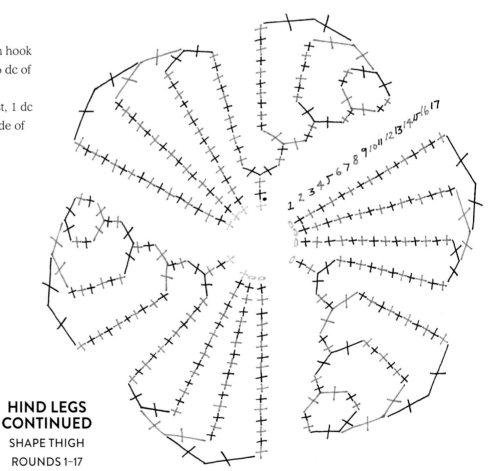

HIND LEGS CONTINUED

SHAPE THIGH

ROUNDS 1–17

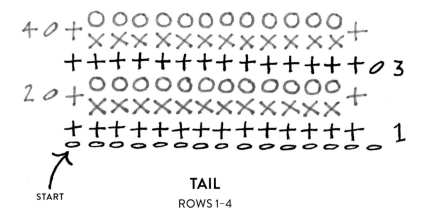

TAIL
ROWS 1–4

START

Tail

With 3.25mm hook and B, make
15 ch. See page 148 for instructions
on loop stitch (lp st).
Row 1: 1 dc in 2nd ch from hook,
1 dc in next 13 ch, turn (14 sts).
Row 2: 1 ch, 1 dc in next dc, 1 lp st
in next 12 dc, 1 dc in next dc, turn.
Row 3: 1 ch, 1 dc in each dc, turn.
Row 4: Rep row 2.
Fasten off, leaving a long tail of yarn
at the end.

Making up

HEAD
Stuff the head. With the tail of yarn
left after fastening off, sew the head
in place, indicated by the marker
at the top of the body. Stitch all
around the neck edges and insert
more stuffing into the neck, if
necessary. With yarn B, embroider
the eyes and nose in satin stitch
(see page 152).

EARS
Turn under one corner of each ear
and stitch to the centre of the ear,
at the lower edge. Sew the ears in
place, near the back of the head,
stitching all around the lower edges.

LEGS
Flatten the top of the legs and sew
in position, stitching all around the
tops of the thighs.

TAIL
Weave the length of yarn left after
fastening off through the stitches
at the narrow end and pull tightly
to gather up the end of the tail.
Fold the tail lengthways and sew
the long edges together with whip
stitch (see page 151). Use the end
of the crochet hook to push a small
amount of stuffing into the tail.
Sew the tail in place. Cut through
the loops.

LONG COAT
The long coat is made by adding
tassels (see page 153) that are
threaded through the posts of the
stitches. Use a single 9½in (24cm)
length of yarn A or B for each tassel.
Attach the tassels to the posts of the
stitches around the head, neck,
body and tops of the legs. Trim the
ends to the desired length. Tie
together a group of tassels above
the eyes into a topknot. Weave in all
the yarn ends.

German Shepherd

METALLIC THREAD IS USED TO EMBROIDER THE NOSE OF THE GERMAN SHEPHERD. THE THREAD HAS A SHINY APPEARANCE THAT STANDS OUT AGAINST THE DARK YARN OF THE MUZZLE.

Materials

- Cascade 220 Superwash, 100% superwash wool (220yd/200m per 100g ball), or any DK yarn:
  1 x 100g ball in 1913 Jet (A)
  1 x 100g ball in 870 Straw (B)
- Approximately 10in (25.5cm) length of metallic stranded embroidery thread for the nose
- 3.25mm (UK10:USD/3) crochet hook
- Blunt-ended yarn needle
- Toy stuffing

Size

- Approximately 9in (23cm) body length from tip of nose to back of hind legs
- Approximately 7½in (19cm) tall from top of head (excluding ears)

Tension

22 sts and 24 rows to 4in (10cm) over double crochet using 3.25mm hook. Use larger or smaller hook if necessary to obtain correct tension.

Method

The German Shepherd's body is worked in rows using two colours. The end of the body is finished in rounds. The legs are worked in continuous rounds of double crochet. The muzzle, head and neck are worked in one piece. The front of the head is crocheted in rounds and top of the head is worked in rows. The neck is crocheted in rounds, first crocheting into the stitches at the underside of the muzzle, and then along the edges of the rows that make up the top of the head. The ears are worked in rows. Each ear is made up of two crocheted parts that are joined by crocheting into each stitch of both pieces at the same time. The tail is worked in double crochet and loop stitch. The loops are cut and brushed to produce the bushy appearance. The long edges of the tail are sewn together and a small amount of stuffing is inserted before sewing it in place. The toes on the paws are produced by crocheting bobbles. The bobbles on the paws appear on the reverse side of the fabric. The eyes and nose are embroidered in satin stitch.

1 ch at beg of the row/round does not count as a st throughout.

Head

Starting at front of muzzle with 3.25mm hook and A, make a magic loop (see page 145).
Round 1: 1 ch, 5 dc into loop (5 sts).
Round 2 (inc): (Dc2inc) 5 times (10 sts). Pull tightly on short end of yarn to close loop.
Round 3: (Dc2inc, 1 dc) 5 times (15 sts).
Rounds 4–7: 1 dc in each dc.

Round 8 (inc): (Dc2inc, 4 dc) 3 times (18 sts).
Rounds 9–10: 1 dc in each dc. Join B in last dc. Continue with B.
Round 11: 1 dc in each dc.
Round 12 (inc): 1 dc in next dc, (dc2inc, 1 dc) 6 times, finishing 5 sts before the end of the round, turn (24 sts).

HEAD
ROUNDS 1–12

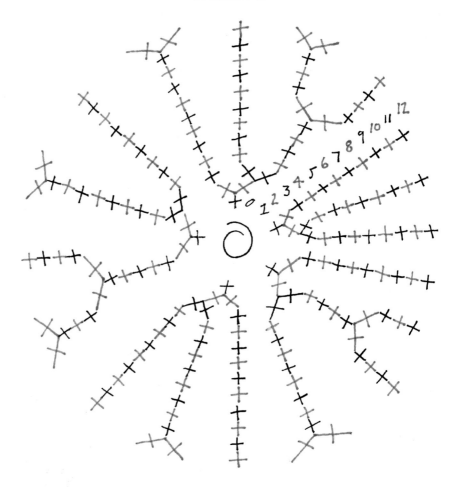

TOP OF HEAD

Row 1 (WS) (inc): 1 dc in next 3 dc, (dc2inc, 2 dc) 5 times, 1 dc in next dc, turn.
Continue on these 24 sts.

Rows 2–6: 1 ch, 1 dc in each dc, turn. Place a marker in the centre of row 5.

Row 7 (dec): (Dc2tog, 2 dc) 6 times, turn (18 sts).

Row 8 (RS) (dec): (Dc2tog, 1 dc) 6 times, turn (12 sts).

Row 9 (dec): (Dc2tog) 6 times (6 sts). Break yarn and thread through last 6 stitches. Pull tightly on end of yarn. Fasten off.

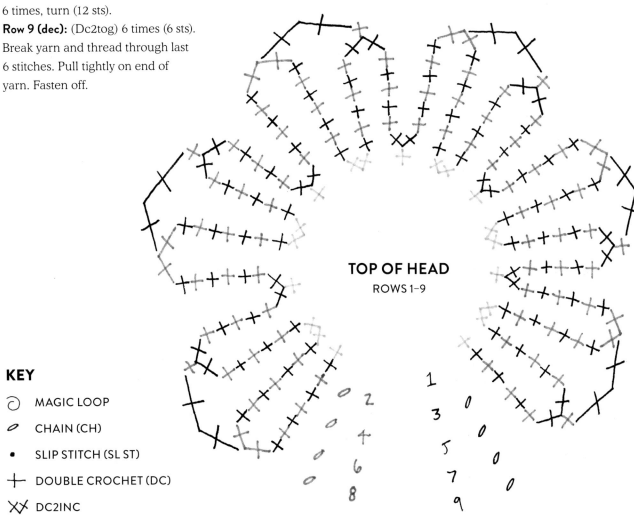

TOP OF HEAD
ROWS 1–9

KEY

- ⟳ MAGIC LOOP
- ᴑ CHAIN (CH)
- • SLIP STITCH (SL ST)
- ┼ DOUBLE CROCHET (DC)
- ⤬ DC2INC
- ⤬ DC2TOG
- ⊖ LOOP STITCH (LP ST)
- ⊕ MAKE BOBBLE (MB)

NECK

With RS of head facing, 3.25mm hook and B, sl st in first of unworked 5 dc of round 12 of head.

Round 1: 1 dc in same st as sl st, 1 dc in next 4 dc, work 16 dc evenly along edge of the rows of head (21 sts).

Rounds 2–5: 1 dc in each dc.

Round 6: (Dc2inc, 1 dc) 4 times, 1 dc in next 13 dc (25 sts).

Rounds 7–8: 1 dc in each dc.

Round 9: 1 dc in next 12 dc, sl st in next st and fasten off, leaving a long tail of yarn at the end.

Ears (make 2)

With 3.25mm hook and B, make 7 ch.

Row 1: 1 dc in 2nd ch from hook, 1 dc in next 4 ch, 3 dc in next ch, 1 dc in reverse side of next 5 ch, turn (13 sts).

Row 2 (inc): 1 ch, dc2inc, 1 dc in next 5 dc, 3 dc in next dc, 1 dc in next 5 dc, dc2inc, turn (17 sts).

Row 3 (inc): 1 ch, dc2inc, 1 dc in next 7 dc, 3 dc in next dc, 1 dc in next 7 dc, dc2inc (21 sts). Fasten off, leaving a long length of yarn at the end. This completes the inner ear. With A, make one more piece to match the first for the outer ear. Turn work at the end and do not fasten off.

JOIN EAR PIECES

Place the two ear pieces together, with the inner ear facing up.

Next: 1 ch, inserting the hook under both loops of each stitch of the inner ear first, then the outer ear at the same time to join, 1 dc in next 10 dc, 3 dc in next dc, 1 dc in next 10 dc (23 sts). Fasten off, leaving a long length of yarn at the end.

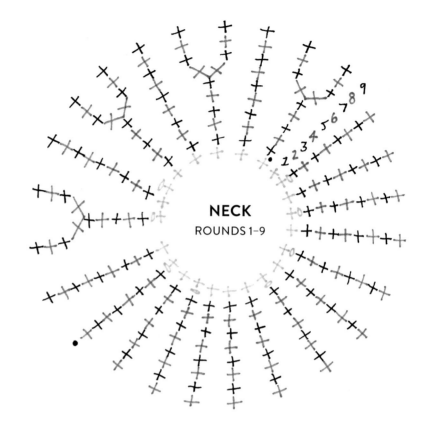

NECK
ROUNDS 1–9

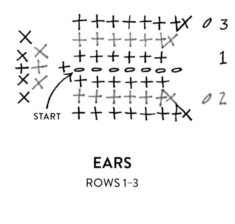

EARS
ROWS 1–3

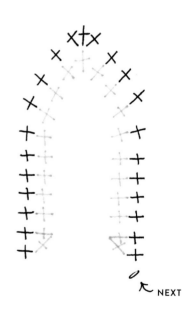

JOIN EAR PIECES
INSERT HOOK INTO EACH STITCH OF BOTH EAR PIECES AT SAME TIME TO JOIN

Body

Starting at front of body, with 3.25mm hook and B, make 10 ch.

Row 1 (RS): 1 dc in 2nd ch from hook, 1 dc in next 7 ch, 2 dc in end ch, 1 dc in reverse side of next 8 ch, turn (18 sts). Place a marker on the first stitch to mark the top of the front of the body.

Row 2 (WS) (inc): 1 ch, (dc2inc, 2 dc) 6 times, sl st in first dc, turn (24 sts).

Row 3 (inc): (Dc2inc, 3 dc) 6 times, turn (30 sts).

Row 4 (inc): 1 ch, (dc2inc, 4 dc) 6 times, sl st in first dc, turn (36 sts).

Row 5 (inc): (Dc2inc, 5 dc) 6 times, turn (42 sts).

Row 6: 1 ch, 1 dc in each dc, sl st in first dc, turn.

Row 7: 1 dc in each dc, turn.

Rows 8–13: Rep last 2 rows 3 times.

Row 14: Rep row 6.

Row 15: 1 dc in next 28 dc. Join A in last dc. With A, work 1 dc in next 14 dc, do not turn.

Next row (RS): With A, work 1 dc in next 14 dc, turn.

BODY
ROWS 1–15 AND NEXT

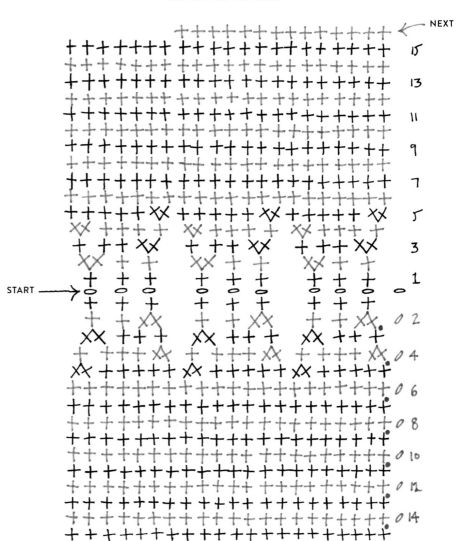

SHAPE MIDDLE OF BODY

Row 1 (WS): 1 ch, 1 dc in next 28 dc with A, 1 dc in next 14 dc with B, sl st in first dc, turn.

Row 2 (RS): 1 dc in next 14 dc with B, 1 dc in next 28 dc with A, turn.

Row 3: Rep row 1.

Row 4 (dec): 1 dc in next 2 dc, dc2tog, 1 dc in next 6 dc, dc2tog, 1 dc in next 2 dc with B, (4 dc, dc2tog) 4 times with A, 1 dc in next 4 dc, turn (36 sts).

Row 5: 1 ch, 1 dc in next 24 dc with A, 1 dc in next 12 dc with B, sl st in first dc, turn.

Row 6: 1 dc in next 12 dc with B, 1 dc in next 24 dc with A, turn.

Rows 7–8: Rep last 2 rows.

Row 9: Rep row 5.

Row 10: (2 dc, dc2tog, 2 dc) twice with B, (2 dc, dc2tog, 2 dc) 4 times with A, turn (30 sts).

Row 11: 1 ch, 1 dc in next 20 dc with A, 1 dc in next 10 dc with B, sl st in first dc, turn.

Row 12: 1 dc in next 10 dc with B, 1 dc in next 20 dc with A, turn.

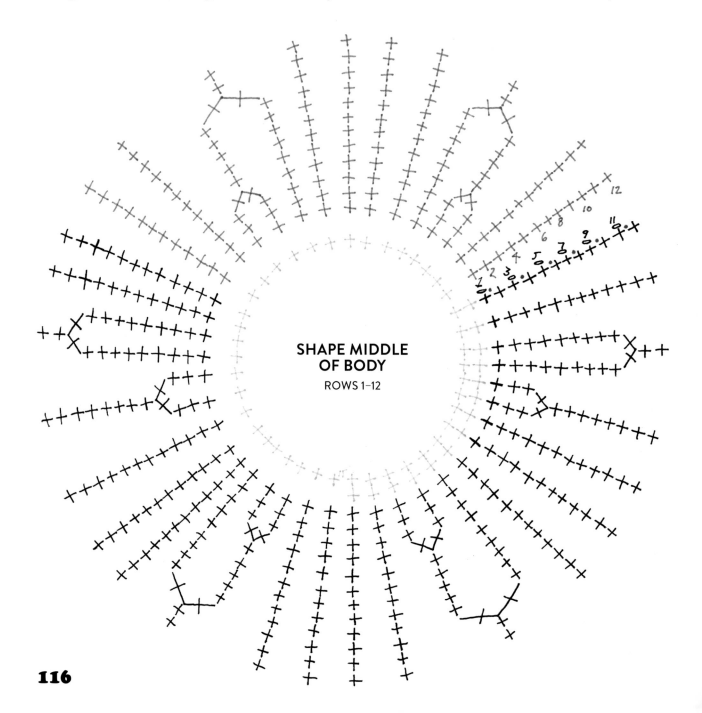

SHAPE MIDDLE OF BODY
ROWS 1–12

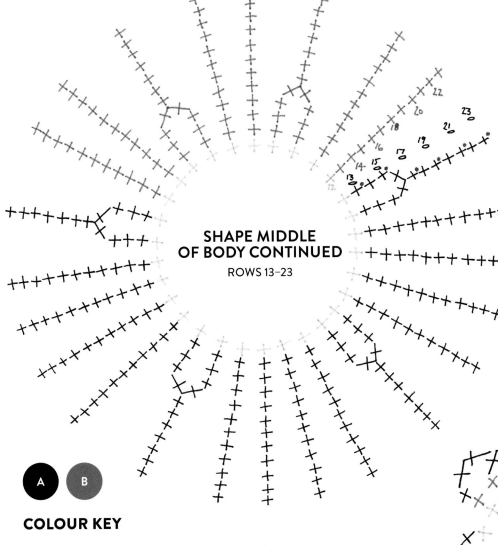

SHAPE MIDDLE
OF BODY CONTINUED
ROWS 13–23

COLOUR KEY

FOR SHAPE MIDDLE AND END OF BODY

A B

SHAPE END OF BODY
ROUNDS 1–3

Rows 13–14: Rep last 2 rows.
Row 15: Rep row 11.
Row 16: 1 dc in next 2 dc, (dc2tog, 2 dc) twice with B, (dc2tog, 4 dc) 3 times with A, dc2tog, turn (24 sts).
Row 17: 1 ch, 1 dc in next 16 dc with A, 1 dc in next 8 dc with B, sl st in first dc, turn.
Row 18: 1 dc in next 8 dc with B, 1 dc in next 16 dc with A, turn.
Rows 19–22: Rep last 2 rows twice.
Row 23: Rep row 17.
Stuff body before continuing.

SHAPE END OF BODY
The following is worked in rounds.
Round 1 (dec): (Dc2tog, 2 dc) twice with B, (dc2tog, 2 dc) 4 times with A (18 sts).
Continue with A.
Round 2 (dec): (Dc2tog, 1 dc) 6 times (12 sts).
Round 3 (dec): (Dc2tog) 6 times (6 sts).
Break yarn and thread through last 6 stitches. Pull tightly on end of yarn to close. Fasten off.

Front legs (make 2)

The bobbles appear on the reverse side of the work. This will be the right side. See page 148 for instructions to make bobble (mb). Starting at the base of the paw, with 3.25mm hook and B, make a magic loop.

Round 1 (WS): 1 ch, 6 dc into loop (6 sts).

Round 2 (inc): (Dc2inc) 6 times (12 sts). Pull tightly on short end of yarn to close loop.

Round 3 (inc): (Dc2inc, 2 dc) 4 times (16 sts).

Round 4: 1 dc in next 8 dc, (mb, 1 dc in next dc) 4 times, turn.

Round 5 (RS) (dec): 1 ch, 1 dc in first dc, (1 dc in next st, dc2tog) twice, 1 dc in next 9 dc (14 sts).

Round 6 (dec): (1 dc in next dc, dc2tog) twice, 1 dc in next 8 dc (12 sts).

Rounds 7–19: 1 dc in each dc.

Round 20 (inc): (Dc2inc, 3 dc) 3 times (15 sts).

Rounds 21–22: 1 dc in each dc.

Round 23 (inc): (Dc2inc, 4 dc) 3 times (18 sts).

Rounds 24–28: 1 dc in each dc. Stuff leg before continuing.

Round 29 (dec): (Dc2tog, 1 dc) 6 times (12 sts).

Round 30 (dec): (Dc2tog) 6 times (6 sts).

Break yarn and thread through last round of stitches. Pull tightly on end of yarn to close. Fasten off, leaving a long tail of yarn at the end.

FRONT LEGS
ROUNDS 1–4

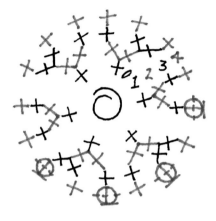

FRONT LEGS CONTINUED
ROUNDS 5–19

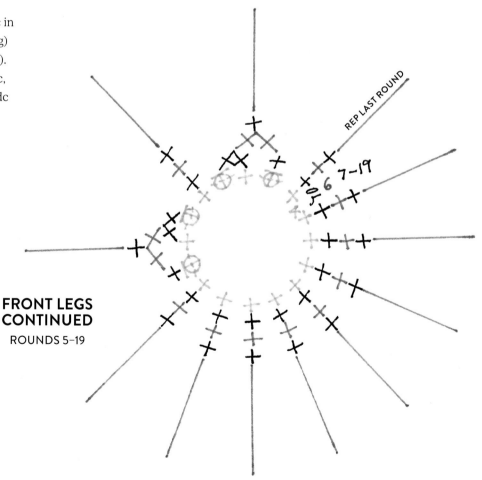

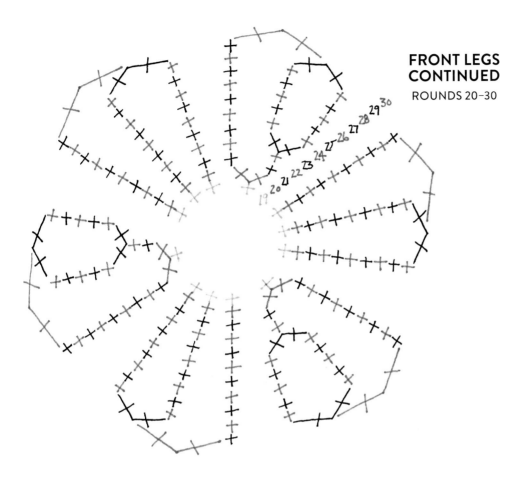

**FRONT LEGS
CONTINUED**
ROUNDS 20–30

Hind legs (make 2)

Starting at the base of the paw,
with 3.25mm hook and B,
make a magic loop.
Rounds 1–15: Work as for rounds
1–15 of front legs.

SHAPE BACK OF LEG

Round 16: 1 dc in next 2 dc, ending
at the side of the leg; 6 ch, skip the
6 dc at the front of the leg, 1 dc in
next 4 dc.
Round 17: 1 dc in next 2 dc, 1 dc in
next 6 ch, 1 dc in next 4 dc.
Break yarn and thread through last
round of stitches. Pull tightly on end
of yarn to close and fasten off.

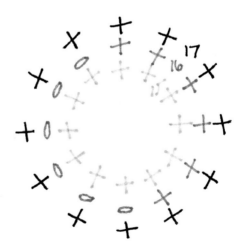

HIND LEGS
SHAPE BACK OF LEG
ROUNDS 16–17

SHAPE THIGH

With RS of leg facing, 3.25mm hook
and B, sl st in first of skipped 6 dc.

Round 1: 1 dc in same st as sl st, 1 dc
in next 5 dc, 1 dc in reverse side of
next 6 ch (12 sts).

Round 2: 1 dc in each dc.

Round 3 (inc): (Dc2inc, 1 dc)
3 times, 1 dc in next 6 dc (15 sts).

Rounds 4–5: 1 dc in each dc.

Round 6 (inc): (Dc2inc, 4 dc) 3 times
(18 sts).

Round 7 (inc): (Dc2inc, 5 dc) 3 times
(21 sts).

Round 8 (inc): (Dc2inc, 6 dc) 3 times
(24 sts).

Rounds 9–17: 1 dc in each dc.
Stuff leg before continuing.

Round 18 (dec): (Dc2tog, 2 dc)
6 times (18 sts).

Round 19 (dec): (Dc2tog, 1 dc)
6 times (12 sts).

Round 20 (dec): (Dc2tog) 6 times
(6 sts).

Break yarn and thread through last
round of stitches. Pull tightly on end
of yarn to close. Fasten off, leaving a
long tail of yarn at the end.

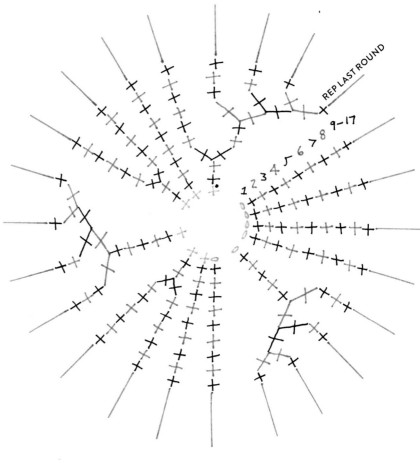

**HIND LEGS
CONTINUED**

SHAPE THIGH

ROUNDS 1–17

**HIND LEGS
CONTINUED**

SHAPE THIGH

ROUNDS 18–20

Tail

The loops appear on the reverse side of the work. This will be the right side. See page 148 for instructions on loop stitch (lp st). With 3.25mm hook and B, make 21 ch.

Row 1: 1 dc in 2nd ch from hook, 1 dc in next 18 ch, 3 dc in end ch, 1 dc in reverse side of next 19 ch, turn (41 sts).

Row 2 (inc): 1 dc in next 2 dc, 1 lp st in next 18 dc, 3 dc in next dc, 1 lp st in next 18 dc, 1 dc in next 2 dc (43 sts).

Join and continue with A.

Row 3 (inc): 1 dc in next 21 sts, dc3inc, 1 dc in next 21 sts, turn (45 sts)

Row 4 (inc): 1 dc in next 2 dc, 1 lp st in next 20 dc, dc3inc, 1 lp st in next 20 dc, 1 dc in next 2 dc, (47 sts). Fasten off, leaving a long tail of yarn at the end.

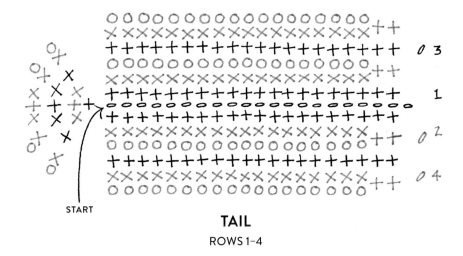

TAIL
ROWS 1–4

Making up

HEAD

Stuff the head. With the tail of yarn left after fastening off, sew the head in place, indicated by the marker at the top of the body. Stitch all around the neck edges. Insert more stuffing into the neck if necessary. With A, embroider the eyes in satin stitch (see page 152). Use metallic embroidery thread to embroider the nose in satin stitch.

EARS

Turn under one corner of each ear and stitch to the centre of the ear, at the lower edge. Sew the ears in place, near the back of the head indicated by the marker, stitching all around the lower edges with the tails of yarn left after fastening off.

LEGS

Flatten the tops of the legs and sew in place, stitching all around the tops of the thighs. Weave in all ends.

TAIL

Using the length of yarn left after fastening off, fold the tail lengthways and sew the long edges together with whip stitch (see page 151), taking care not to catch the loops in the stitches. Use the end of the crochet hook to push a small amount of stuffing into the tail. Cut through the loops and brush the strands of yarn to fluff them. Sew the tail to the end of the body.

Poodle

A COMBINATION OF DOUBLE CROCHET AND CHAIN STITCHES FORM THE CLIPPED COAT OF THIS PAMPERED WHITE POODLE. CHOOSE A DIFFERENT COLOUR, IF DESIRED, TO MAKE YOUR OWN BEST IN SHOW AWARD WINNER.

Materials

- Rowan Pure Wool Superwash DK, 100% wool (137yd/125m per 50g ball), or any DK yarn: 2 x 50g balls in 012 Snow (A)
- Approximately 20in (51cm) length of black DK yarn, such as 114 Caviar (B)
- 3.25mm (UK10:USD/3) crochet hook
- Blunt-ended yarn needle
- Toy stuffing

Size

- Approximately 6¾in (17cm) body length
- Approximately 10⅝in (27cm) tall from top of head

Tension

22 sts and 26 rows to 4in (10cm) over double crochet using 3.25mm hook. Use larger or smaller hook if necessary to obtain correct tension.

Method

The poodle is worked in continuous rounds. The muzzle, head and neck are worked in one piece. The body, legs and tail are crocheted separately and the pieces are sewn together after stuffing. The stitch that forms the curly coat is made by crocheting a number of chain stitches, then working a slip stitch into the front loops only of the previous row, so the chains appear on the right side of the fabric. The toes on the paws are produced by crocheting bobbles. These appear on the reverse side of the fabric, so the work is turned before continuing with the leg. The eyes and nose are embroidered in black yarn.

1 ch at beg of the row/round does not count as a st throughout.

Head

Starting at front of muzzle, with 3.25mm hook and A, make a magic loop (see page 145).

Round 1: 1 ch, 6 dc into loop (6 sts).
Round 2 (inc): (Dc2inc) 6 times (12 sts). Pull tightly on short end of yarn to close loop.
Rounds 3–4: 1 dc in each dc.
Round 5 (inc): (Dc2inc, 3 dc) 3 times (15 sts).
Rounds 6–8: 1 dc in each dc.
Round 9 (inc): (Dc2inc, 4 dc) 3 times (18 sts).
Rounds 10–12: 1 dc in each dc.

DIVIDE FOR NECK

Round 13: 12 ch, skip next 6 dc, 1 dc in next 12 dc.
Round 14: Dc in next 12 ch, 1 dc in next 12 dc (24 sts).

TOP OF HEAD

Round 15: 1 dc in each dc.
Round 16 (inc): (Dc2inc, 3 dc) 6 times (30 sts).
Round 17 (inc): (Dc2inc, 4 dc) 6 times (36 sts).
Round 18: Working in front loop only of each st, (sl st in next st, 6 ch, sl st in next 2 sts) 12 times (12 6-ch loops).

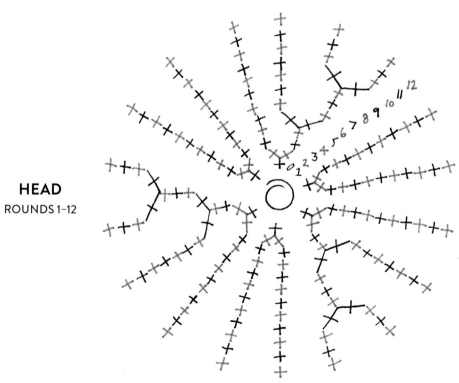

HEAD
ROUNDS 1–12

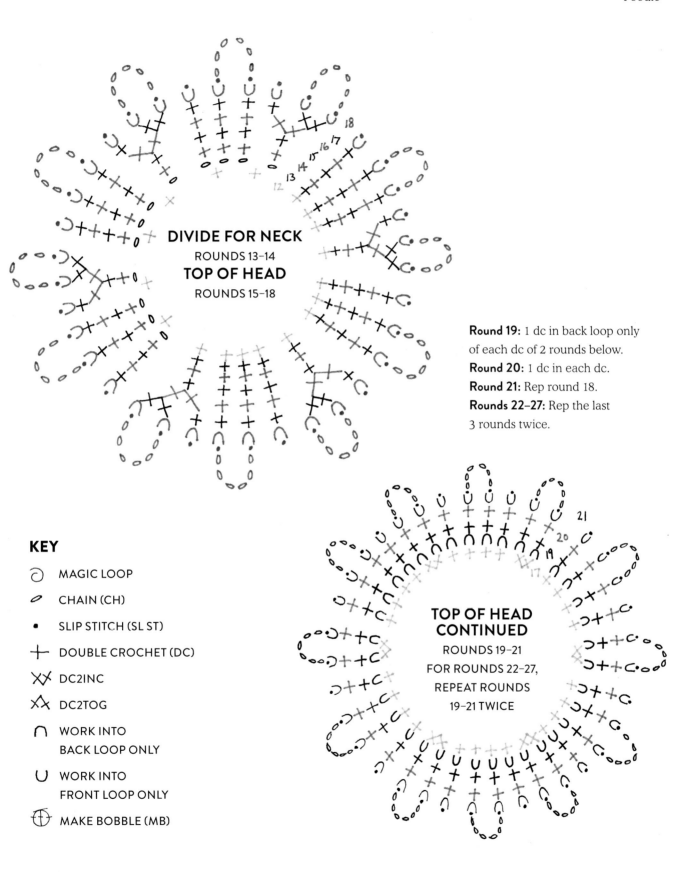

DIVIDE FOR NECK
ROUNDS 13–14
TOP OF HEAD
ROUNDS 15–18

Round 19: 1 dc in back loop only
of each dc of 2 rounds below.
Round 20: 1 dc in each dc.
Round 21: Rep round 18.
Rounds 22–27: Rep the last
3 rounds twice.

KEY

⌒ MAGIC LOOP

⊘ CHAIN (CH)

• SLIP STITCH (SL ST)

+ DOUBLE CROCHET (DC)

⋇ DC2INC

⋏ DC2TOG

∩ WORK INTO
BACK LOOP ONLY

U WORK INTO
FRONT LOOP ONLY

⊕ MAKE BOBBLE (MB)

**TOP OF HEAD
CONTINUED**
ROUNDS 19–21
FOR ROUNDS 22–27,
REPEAT ROUNDS
19–21 TWICE

125

Round 28 (dec): Working in back loop only of each st of 2 rounds below, (dc2tog, 4 dc) 6 times (30 sts).

Round 29 (dec): (Dc2tog, 3 dc) 6 times (24 sts).

Round 30: Working in front loop only of each st, (sl st in next st, 6 ch, sl st in next 2 sts) 8 times (8 6-ch loops).

Round 31 (dec): Working in back loop only of each st of 2 rounds below, (dc2tog, 2 dc) 6 times (18 sts).

Round 32 (dec): (Dc2tog) 9 times (9 sts).

Round 33: Working in front loop only of each st, (sl st in next st, 6 ch, sl st in next 2 sts) 3 times (3 6-ch loops).

Round 34: 1 dc in back loop only of each dc of 2 rounds below. Break yarn and thread through last round of stitches. Pull tightly on end of yarn to close. Fasten off.

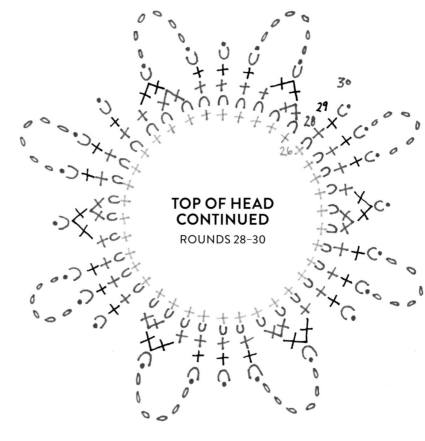

TOP OF HEAD CONTINUED
ROUNDS 28–30

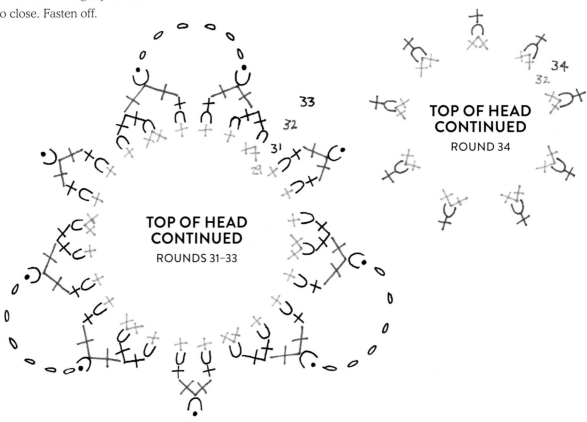

TOP OF HEAD CONTINUED
ROUNDS 31–33

TOP OF HEAD CONTINUED
ROUND 34

NECK

Turn the head upside down and, with RS facing and 3.25mm hook, join A with a sl st to first of skipped 6 dc of round 12 of head.

Round 1: 1 dc in same st as sl st, 1 dc in next 5 dc, 1 dc in reverse side of next 12 ch of row 13 of head (18 sts).

Rounds 2–6: 1 dc in each dc. Sl st in next st and fasten off, leaving a long tail of yarn at the end.

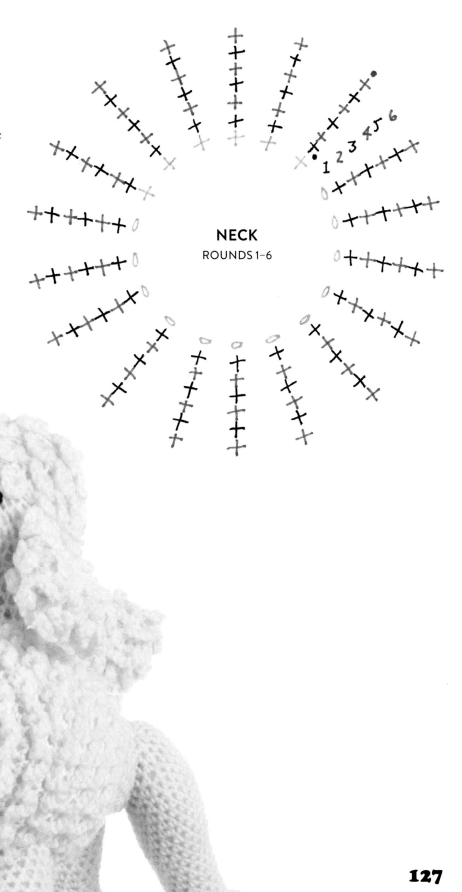

NECK
ROUNDS 1–6

Ears (make 2)

With 3.25mm hook and A, make 10 ch.

Round 1: 1 dc in 2nd ch from hook, 1 dc in next 7 ch, 2 dc in end ch, 1 dc in reverse side of next 8 ch (18 sts).

Round 2: Working in front loop only of each st, (sl st in next st, 6 ch, sl st in next 2 sts) 6 times (6 6-ch loops).

Round 3 (inc): Working in back loop only of each st of 2 rounds below, (dc2inc, 2 dc) 6 times (24 sts).

Round 4 (inc): (Dc2inc, 3 dc) 6 times (30 sts).

Round 5: Working in back loop only of each st, (sl st in next st, 6 ch, sl st in next 2 sts) 10 times (10 6-ch loops).

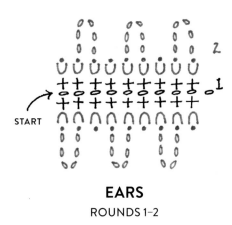

EARS
ROUNDS 1–2

START

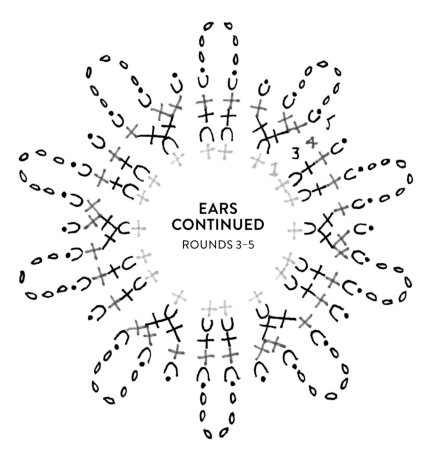

EARS CONTINUED
ROUNDS 3–5

Round 6: 1 dc in back loop only
of each dc of 2 rounds below.
Round 7: 1 dc in each dc.
Round 8: Rep round 5.
Round 9 (dec): Working in back loop
only of each st of 2 rounds below,
(dc2tog, 3 dc) 6 times (24 sts).
Round 10 (dec): (Dc2tog, 2 dc)
6 times (18 sts).
Round 11: Rep round 2.

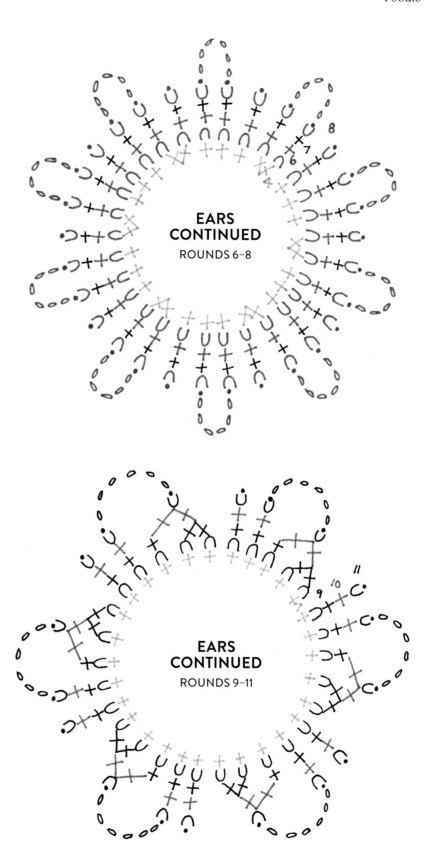

EARS
CONTINUED
ROUNDS 6–8

EARS
CONTINUED
ROUNDS 9–11

Round 12: 1 dc in back loop only of each dc of 2 rounds below.

Round 13: 1 dc in each dc.

Round 14: Rep round 2.

Round 15 (dec): Working in back loop only of each st of 2 rounds below, (dc2tog, 1 dc) 6 times (12 sts).

Round 16: 1 dc in each dc.

Round 17: Working in front loop only of each st, (sl st in next st, 6 ch, sl st in next 2 sts) 4 times (4 6-ch loops).

Round 18: 1 dc in back loop only of each dc of 2 rounds below. Sl st and fasten off, leaving a long tail of yarn at the end.

EARS CONTINUED
ROUNDS 12–14

EARS CONTINUED
ROUNDS 15–17

EARS CONTINUED
ROUND 18

Body

Starting at rear end, with 3.25mm hook and A, make a magic loop.

Round 1: 1 ch, 6 dc into loop (6 sts).

Round 2 (inc): (Dc2inc) 6 times (12 sts). Pull tightly on short end of yarn to close loop.

Round 3 (inc): (Dc2inc, 1 dc) 6 times (18 sts).

Round 4 (inc): (Dc2inc, 2 dc) 6 times (24 sts).

Rounds 5–20: 1 dc in each dc.

Round 21: Working in front loop only of each st, (sl st in next st, 6 ch, sl st in next 2 sts) 8 times (8 6-ch loops).

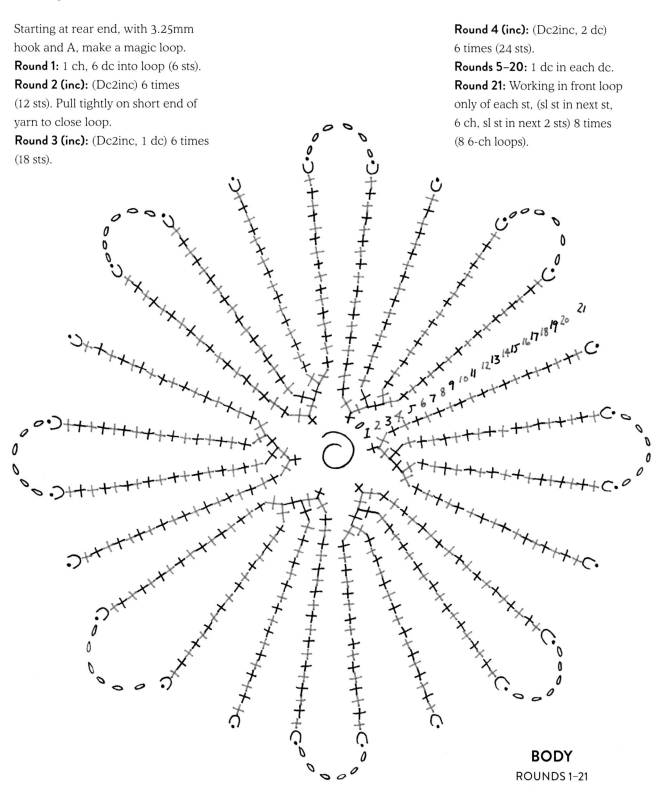

BODY
ROUNDS 1–21

Round 22 (inc): Working in back loop only of each st of 2 rounds below, (dc2inc, 3 dc) 6 times (30 sts).

Round 23 (inc): (Dc2inc, 4 dc) 6 times (36 sts).

Round 24: Working in front loop only of each st, (sl st in next st, 6 ch, sl st in next 2 sts) 12 times (12 6-ch loops).

Round 25 (inc): Working in back loop only of each st of 2 rounds below, (dc2inc, 5 dc) 6 times (42 sts).

Round 26 (inc): (Dc2inc, 6 dc) 6 times (48 sts).

Round 27: Working in front loop only of each st, (sl st in next st, 6 ch, sl st in next 2 sts) 16 times (16 6-ch loops).

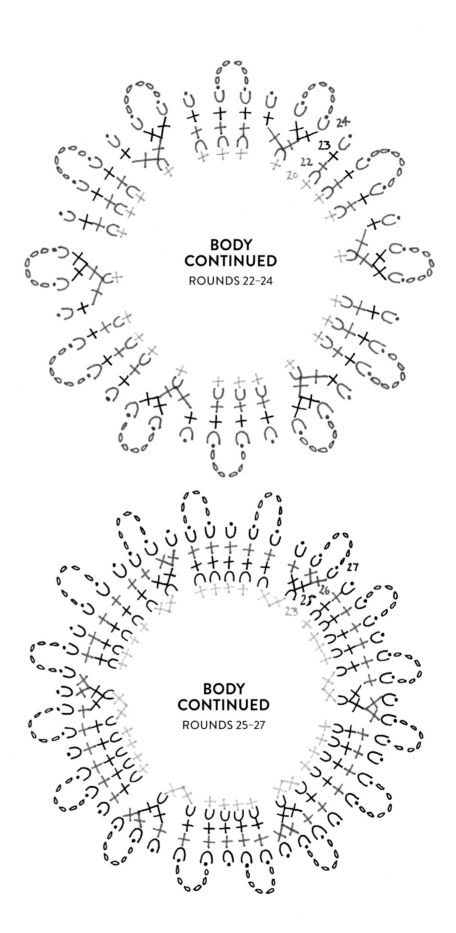

BODY CONTINUED
ROUNDS 22–24

BODY CONTINUED
ROUNDS 25–27

Round 28: 1 dc in back loop only of each dc of 2 rounds below.

Round 29: 1 dc in each dc.

Round 30: Rep round 27.

Rounds 31–48: Rep the last 3 rounds 6 times.

Round 49 (dec): Working in back loop only of each st of 2 rounds below, (dc2tog, 6 dc) 6 times (42 sts).

Round 50 (dec): (Dc2tog, 5 dc) 6 times (36 sts).

Round 51: Rep round 24.

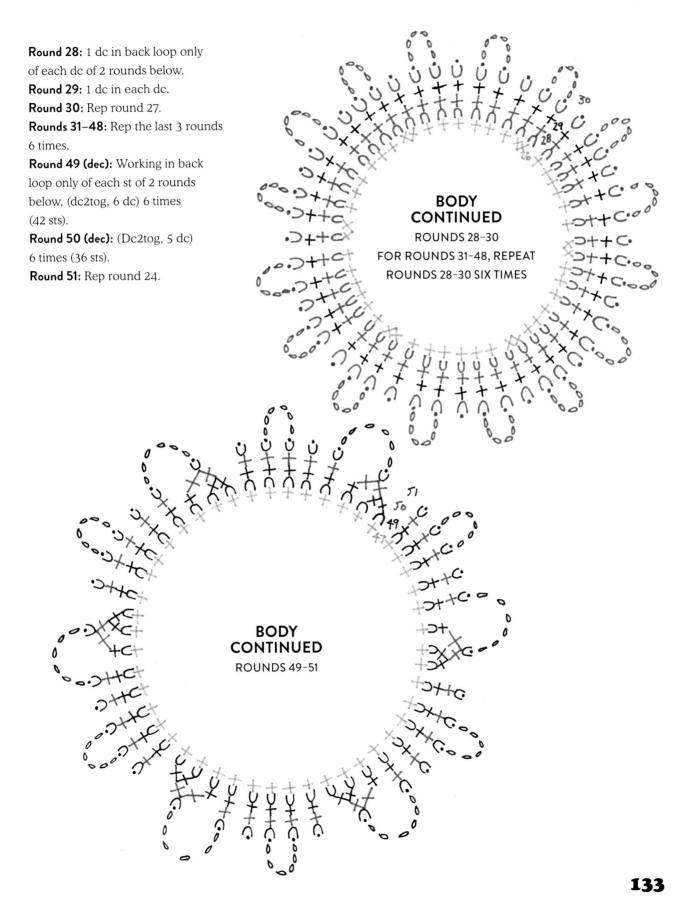

BODY CONTINUED

ROUNDS 28–30

FOR ROUNDS 31–48, REPEAT ROUNDS 28–30 SIX TIMES

BODY CONTINUED

ROUNDS 49–51

133

Round 52 (dec): Working in back loop only of each st of 2 rounds below, (dc2tog, 4 dc) 6 times (30 sts).

Round 53 (dec): (Dc2tog, 3 dc) 6 times (24 sts).

Round 54: Rep round 21. Stuff body to within the last few rounds before continuing.

Rounds 55–58: Work as for rounds 31–34 of head, inserting more stuffing, if necessary, before the last 2 rounds.

Break yarn and thread through last round of stitches. Pull tightly on end of yarn to close. Fasten off.

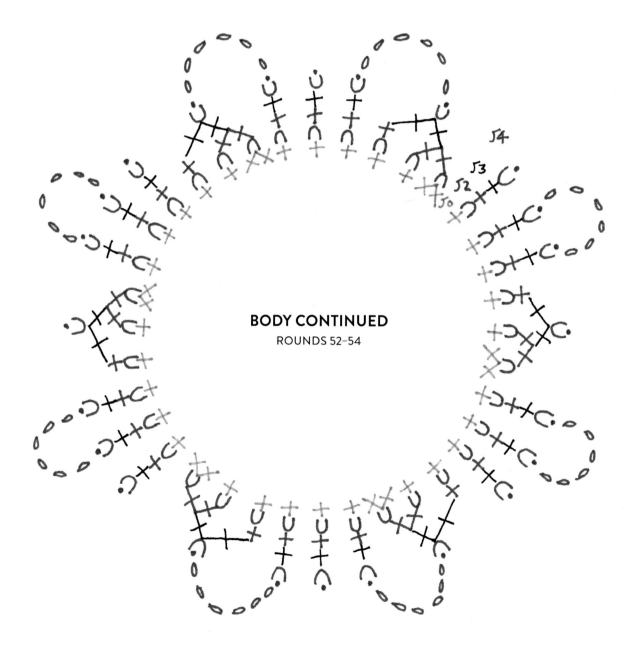

BODY CONTINUED
ROUNDS 52–54

Front legs (make 2)

The bobbles appear on the reverse side of the work. This will be the right side. See page 148 for instructions to make bobble (mb). Starting at the base of the paw, with 3.25mm hook and A, make a magic loop.

Round 1 (WS): 1 ch, 6 dc into loop (6 sts).

Round 2 (inc): (Dc2inc) 6 times (12 sts). Pull tightly on short end of yarn to close loop.

Round 3 (inc): (Dc2inc, 2 dc) 4 times (16 sts).

Round 4: 1 dc in next 8 dc, (mb, 1 dc in next dc) 4 times, turn.

Round 5 (RS) (dec): 1 ch, 1 dc in first dc, (1 dc in next dc, dc2tog) twice, 1 dc in next 9 dc (14 sts).

Round 6 (dec): (1 dc in next dc, dc2tog) twice, 1 dc in next 8 dc (12 sts).

Rounds 7–9: 1 dc in each dc.

Round 10: Working in front loop only of each st, (sl st in next st, 6 ch, sl st in next 2 sts) 4 times (4 6-ch loops).

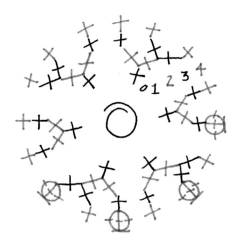

FRONT LEGS
ROUNDS 1–4

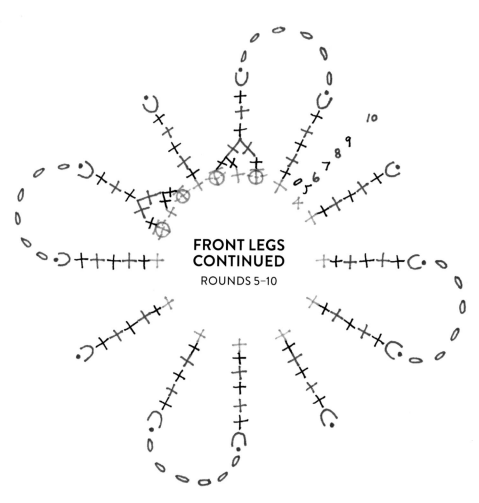

FRONT LEGS CONTINUED
ROUNDS 5–10

Round 11 (inc): Working in back loop only of each st of 2 rounds below, (dc2inc, 1 dc) 6 times (18 sts).
Round 12 (inc): (Dc2inc, 2 dc) 6 times (24 sts).
Round 13: Working in front loop only of each st, (sl st in next st, 6 ch, sl st in next 2 sts) 8 times (8 6-ch loops).
Round 14: 1 dc in back loop only of each dc of 2 rounds below.
Round 15: 1 dc in each dc.
Round 16: Rep round 13.
Rounds 17–19: Rep last 3 rounds.

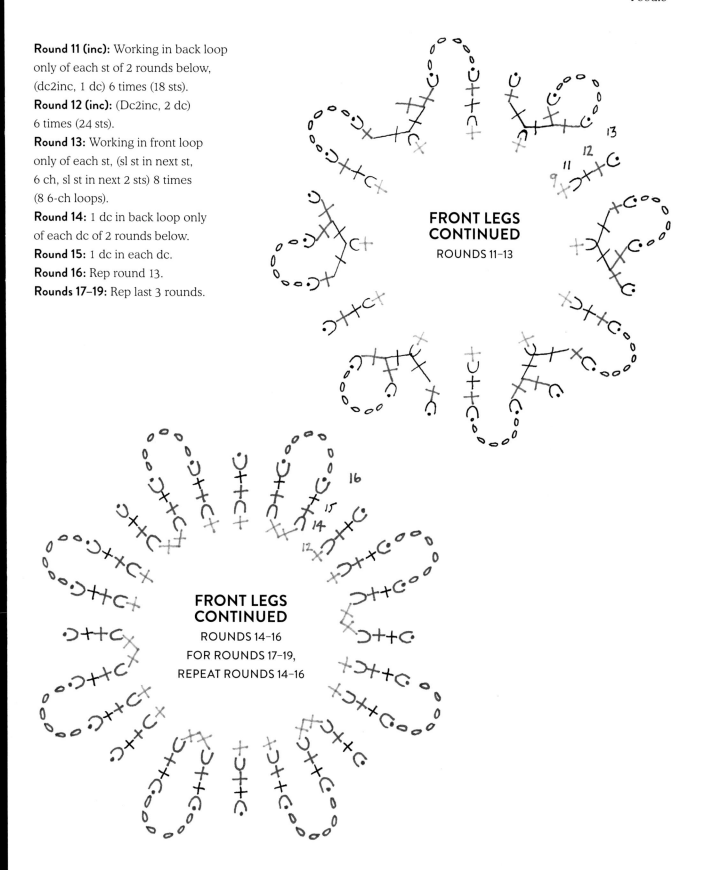

FRONT LEGS CONTINUED
ROUNDS 11–13

FRONT LEGS CONTINUED
ROUNDS 14–16
FOR ROUNDS 17–19,
REPEAT ROUNDS 14–16

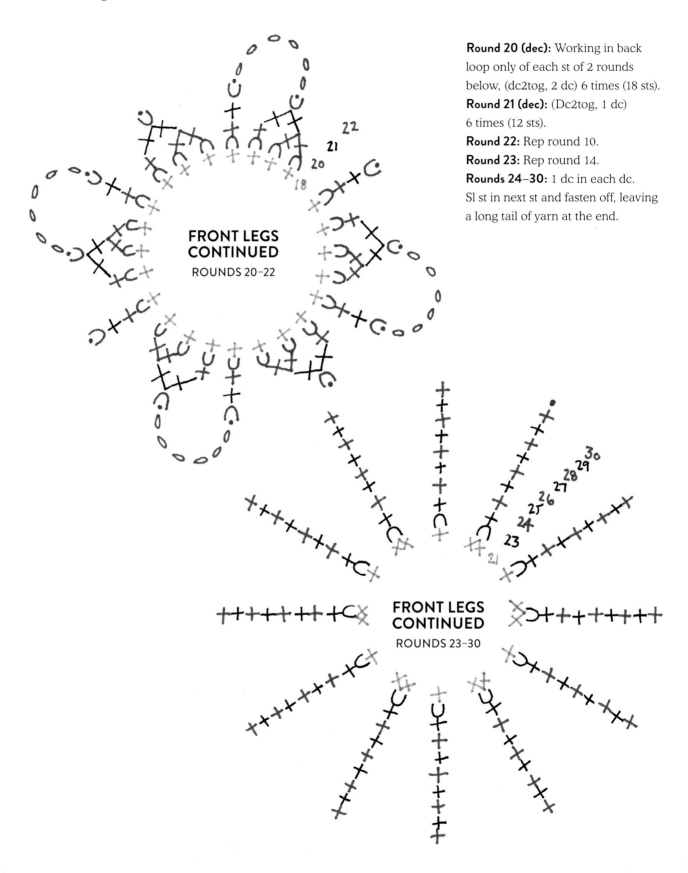

FRONT LEGS CONTINUED
ROUNDS 20–22

FRONT LEGS CONTINUED
ROUNDS 23–30

Round 20 (dec): Working in back loop only of each st of 2 rounds below, (dc2tog, 2 dc) 6 times (18 sts).
Round 21 (dec): (Dc2tog, 1 dc) 6 times (12 sts).
Round 22: Rep round 10.
Round 23: Rep round 14.
Rounds 24–30: 1 dc in each dc. Sl st in next st and fasten off, leaving a long tail of yarn at the end.

Hind legs (make 2)

Starting at the base of the paw, with 3.25mm hook and A, make a magic loop.

Rounds 1–27: Work as for rounds 1–27 of front legs.

Round 28 (inc): (Dc2inc, 3 dc) 3 times (15 sts).

Rounds 29–31: 1 dc in each dc.

Round 32 (inc): (Dc2inc, 4 dc) 3 times (18 sts).

Rounds 33–35: 1 dc in each dc.

Round 36 (inc): (Dc2inc, 5 dc) 3 times (21 sts).

Rounds 37–39: 1 dc in each dc. Stuff leg before continuing.

HIND LEGS
ROUNDS 28–39

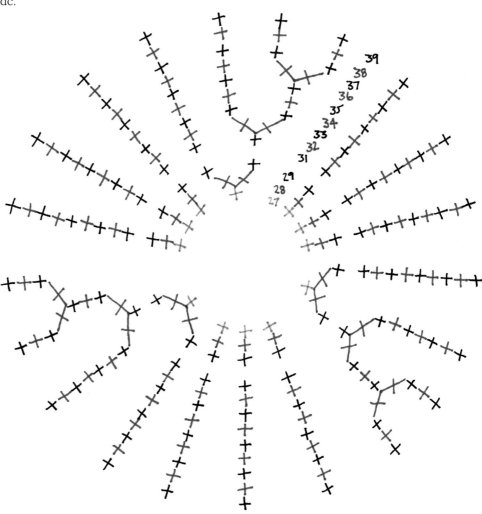

Round 40 (dec): (Dc2tog, 5 dc)
3 times (18 sts).
Round 41: 1 dc in each dc.
Round 42 (dec): (Dc2tog, 4 dc)
3 times (15 sts).
Round 43: 1 dc in each dc.
Round 44 (dec): (Dc2tog, 3 dc)
3 times (12 sts).
Add more stuffing before
continuing.
Round 45 (dec): (Dc2tog) 6 times
(6 sts).
Break yarn and thread through last
round of stitches. Pull tightly on end
of yarn to close. Fasten off, leaving
a long tail of yarn at the end.

Tail

With 3.25mm hook and A, make
a magic loop.
Round 1: 1 ch, 6 dc into loop (6 sts).
Round 2: 1 dc in back loop only of
each dc. Pull tightly on short end of
yarn to close loop.
Rounds 3–6: 1 dc in each dc.
Round 7 (inc): (Dc2inc) 6 times
(12 sts).
Rounds 8–18: Work as for rounds
10–20 of front legs.
Stuff tail, using the end of the
crochet hook to push the stuffing
into the narrow end of the tail.
Rounds 19–21: Work as for rounds
32–34 of head.
Break yarn and thread through last
round of stitches. Pull tightly on end
of yarn to close. Fasten off.

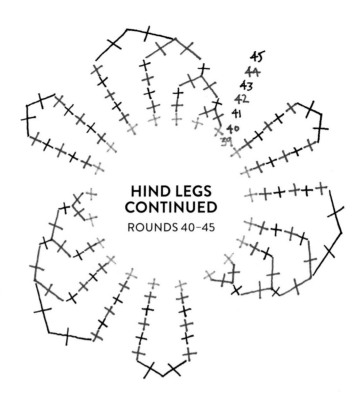

**HIND LEGS
CONTINUED**
ROUNDS 40–45

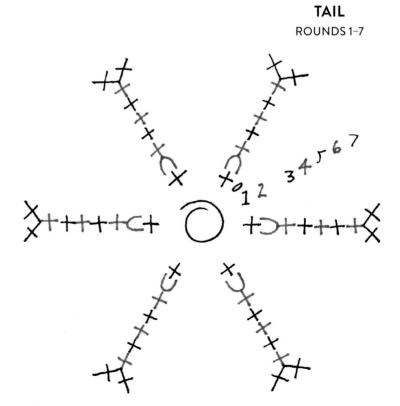

TAIL
ROUNDS 1–7

Making up

HEAD

Stuff the head. Use the tail of yarn left after fastening off to sew the head to the body, stitching all around the neck. Tuck the chain loops that will be covered by the head inside the neck and take care not to catch the loops that appear around the outside edges of the neck in the stitches. Insert more stuffing into the neck if necessary. Embroider eyes and nose in satin stitch (see page 152) with yarn B.

EARS

Flatten the ear and sew together the six stitches from each side of the last round to form a straight seam. Sew an ear to each side of the head, under the first round of chain loops.

LEGS

Stuff the front legs and sew them in place, tucking the chain loops in that will be covered and taking care not to catch the rest of the loops in the stitches. Flatten the tops of the back legs and sew in position, stitching around the top of the thighs.

TAIL

Sew the tail in place, stitching through the front loops of stitches of the first round to attach it to the poodle. Weave in the short ends of yarn.

Getting Started

YOU WILL FIND EVERYTHING YOU WILL NEED TO MAKE YOUR CROCHETED DOG IN THE LIST OF MATERIALS AT THE BEGINNING OF EACH PATTERN.

Hooks

Crochet hook sizes vary widely, from tiny hooks that produce a very fine stitch when used with threads, to oversized hooks for working with several strands of yarn at one time to create a bulky fabric. Using a larger or smaller hook will change the look of the fabric; it will also affect the tension and the amount of yarn required. The projects in this book use just two sizes: 3.25mm (UK10:USD/3) and 3.5mm (UK9:USE/4).

Needles

A blunt-ended yarn needle is used to sew the projects together. The large eye makes it easy to thread the needle and the rounded end will prevent any snagging.

Substituting yarns

When substituting yarns, it is important to calculate the number of balls required by the number of yards or metres per ball rather than the weight of the yarn, because this varies according to the fibre. Tension is also important. Always work a tension swatch in the yarn you wish to use before starting a project.

Reading charts

Each symbol on a chart represents a stitch; each round or row represents one round or row of crochet.

For rounds of crochet, read the chart anti-clockwise, starting at the centre and working out to the last round on the chart.

For rows of crochet, the chart should be read back and forth, following the number at the beginning of each row.

The charts are shown in alternate rounds or rows of blue and black. The last round or row from a previous chart is shown in grey. Where multiple colour changes are used, the stitches on the charts are shown in the colour to represent each yarn.

Tension

It is vital to check your tension before starting a project, as this will affect the size and look of the dog, as well as the amount of yarn you will use. The tension is the number of rows and stitches per square inch or centimetre of crocheted fabric. Using the same size hook and type of stitch as in the pattern, work a sample of around 5in (12.5cm) square and then smooth out on a flat surface.

STITCHES

Place a ruler horizontally across the work and mark 4in (10cm) with pins. Count the number of stitches between the pins, including half stitches. This will give you the tension of stitches.

ROWS

Measure the tension of rows by placing a ruler vertically over the work and mark 4in (10cm) with pins. Count the number of rows between the pins.

If the number of stitches and rows is greater than those stated in the pattern, your tension is tighter and you should use a larger hook. If the number of stitches and rows is fewer than those stated in the pattern, your tension is looser, so you should use a smaller hook.

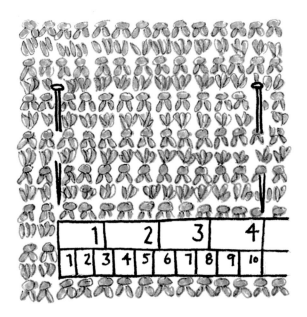

STITCHES

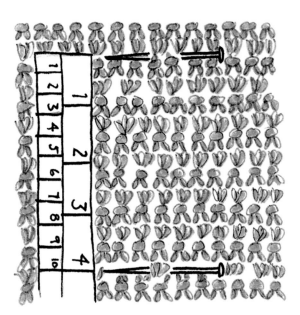

ROWS

Crochet Stitches

HERE YOU WILL FIND THE BASIC INFORMATION ON HOW TO HOLD THE HOOK AND YARN, CROCHETING THE VARIOUS STITCHES AND JOINING IN A NEW COLOUR.

Slip knot

Take the end of the yarn and form it into a loop. Holding it in place between thumb and forefinger, insert the hook through the loop, catch the long end that is attached to the ball, and draw it back through. Keeping the yarn looped on the hook, pull through until the loop closes around the hook, ensuring it is not tight. Pulling on the short end of yarn will loosen the knot, while pulling on the long end will tighten it.

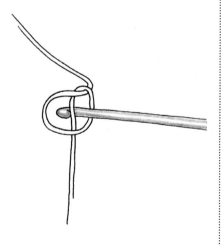

SLIP KNOT

Holding the work

HOOK

Hold the hook as you would a pencil, bringing your middle finger forwards to rest near the tip of the hook. This will help control the movement of the hook, while the fingers of your other hand will regulate the tension of the yarn. The hook should face you, pointing slightly downwards. The motion of the hook and yarn should be free and even, not tight. This will come with practice.

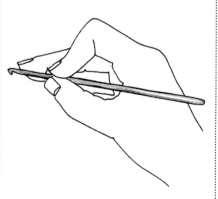

HOLDING THE HOOK

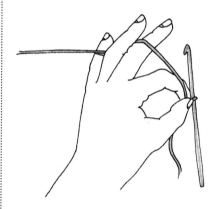

HOLDING THE YARN

YARN

To hold your work and control the tension, pass the yarn over the first two fingers of your left hand (right if you are left-handed), under the third finger and around the little finger, and let the yarn fall loosely to the ball. As you work, take the stitch you made between the thumb and forefinger of the same hand. The hook is usually inserted through the top two loops of a stitch as you work, unless otherwise stated in a pattern. A different effect is produced when only the back or front loop of the stitch is picked up.

Magic loop

Many of the crocheted pieces start with an adjustable loop of yarn. To make the loop, wind the yarn around a finger, insert the hook, catch the yarn and draw back through the loop. After a couple of rounds have been crocheted, covering the loop of yarn, the short end of yarn is pulled tight to close the centre. An alternative method is to make four chain stitches and then slip stitch to the first chain to form a ring. However, this technique does leave a hole in the middle.

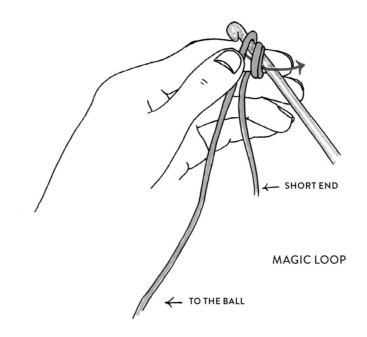

← SHORT END

MAGIC LOOP

← TO THE BALL

Chain (ch)

1 Pass the hook under and over the yarn that is held taut between the first and second fingers. This is called 'yarn round hook' (yrh). Draw the yarn through the loop on the hook. This makes one chain (ch).

2 Repeat step 1, keeping the thumb and forefinger of the left hand close to the hook, until you have as many chain stitches as required.

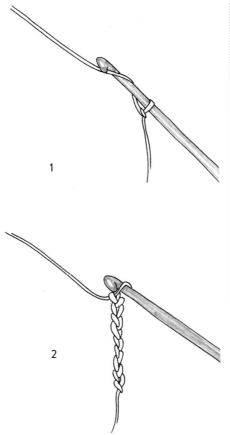

1

2

Slip stitch (sl st)

Make a practice chain of 10. Insert hook into first stitch (st), yrh, draw through both loops on hook. This forms one slip stitch (sl st). Continue to end. This will give you 10 slip stitches (10 sts).

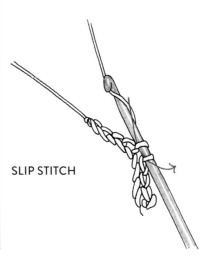

SLIP STITCH

145

Double crochet (dc)

Make a practice chain of 17.
Skip the first ch.

1 Insert hook from front into the next stitch, yrh and draw back through the stitch (two loops on hook).

2 Yrh and draw through two loops (one loop on hook). This makes one double crochet (dc).

Repeat steps 1 and 2 to the end of the row. On the foundation chain of 17 sts you should have 16 double crochet sts (16 sts).

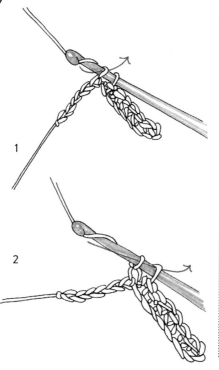

NEXT ROW

Turn the work so the reverse side faces you. Make 1 ch. This is the turning chain; it helps keep a neat edge and does not count as a stitch. Rep steps 1 and 2 to the end of the row. Continue until the desired number of rows is complete. Fasten off.

Fastening off

When you have finished, fasten off by cutting the yarn around 4¾in (12cm) from the work. Draw the loose end through the remaining loop, pulling it tightly.

Half treble (htr)

Make a practice chain of 17.
Skip the first 2 ch (these count as the first half treble stitch).

1 Yrh, insert hook into the next stitch, yrh and draw back through stitch (three loops on hook).

2 Yrh, draw through all three loops (one loop on hook). This forms 1 half treble (htr).

Repeat steps 1 and 2 to the end of the row.

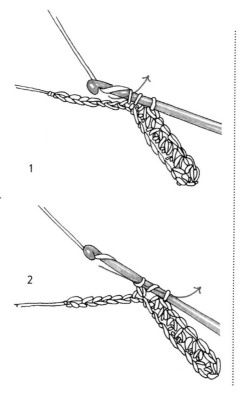

On the foundation chain of 17 sts, you should have 16 half trebles (16 sts), including the 2 ch at the beginning of the row, which is counted as the first stitch.

NEXT ROW

Turn the work so the reverse side faces you. Make 2 ch to count as the first half treble. Skip the first stitch of the previous row. Repeat steps 1 and 2 for the next 14 htr of the last row, work 1 htr in the second of the 2 ch at the end of the row. Continue until the desired number of rows is complete. Fasten off.

Treble (tr)

Make a practice chain of 18. Skip the first 3 ch stitches (these count as the first tr).

1 Yrh, insert hook into the next stitch, yrh and draw back through the stitch (three loops on hook).

2 Yrh, draw through two loops (two loops on hook).

3 Yrh, draw through two loops (one loop on hook). This forms 1 treble (tr).

Repeat steps 1–3 to end of row. On the foundation chain of 18 sts you should have 16 trebles (16 sts), including the 3 ch at the beginning of the row, which is counted as the first stitch.

NEXT ROW

Turn the work so the reverse side faces you. Make 3 ch to count as the first treble. Skip the first stitch of the previous row. Repeat steps 1–3 to the end of the row, working 1 tr into the third of the 3 ch at the beginning of the last row. Continue until the desired number of rows is complete. Fasten off.

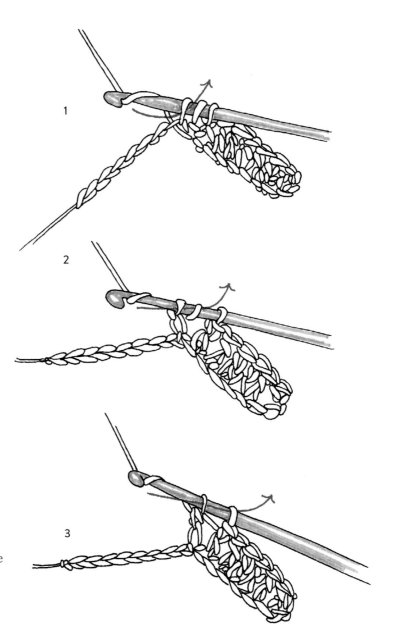

Make bobble (mb)

This stitch is used to create the toes on the dogs' paws. The bobbles appear on the reverse side of the work. This will be the right side.

1–2 Follow steps 1–2 of treble stitch.

3 *Yrh, insert hook into same st, yrh and draw back through stitch (four loops on hook), yrh and draw through two loops (three loops on hook)*; rep from * to * (four loops on hook) yrh, draw through all four loops (one loop on hook). This forms one bobble.

Loop stitch (lp st)

The loops appear on the reverse side of the work. This will be the right side. This method is used to create the ears and feathered coat of the Spaniel on pages 93–4. The same stitch is used on the Yorkshire Terrier's tail on page 109. The loops are cut, producing single strands of yarn to form the long hair on the tail. Insert hook into next dc, with yarn wrapped around the finger of the yarn hand (see 'Holding the work', page 144), from front to back. Catch the strand at the back of the finger and the strand at the front at the same time, and draw both strands of yarn through the stitch (three loops on hook). Slip loop off finger, yrh and draw through all three loops on hook.

Increasing

To increase one double crochet (dc2inc), work two stitches into one stitch of the previous row. To increase two double crochet stitches (dc3inc), work three stitches into one stitch of the previous row.

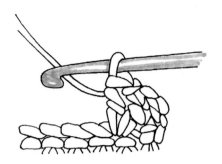

Decreasing

To decrease one double crochet (dc2tog), insert the hook into the next st, yrh and draw back through the stitch (two loops on hook); insert the hook into the following st, yrh and draw back through the st (three loops on hook), yrh and draw through all three loops on the hook.

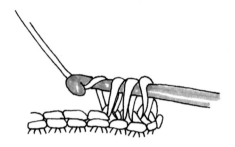

LOOP STITCH

Working into the back or front loop only

The front loop of a stitch is the one closer to you; the back loop is the stitch further away. Generally, the hook is inserted into both loops of a stitch, but when only one loop is crocheted into, the horizontal bar of the remaining loop is left on the surface of the fabric. This method is used on the French Bulldog's muzzle on page 42.

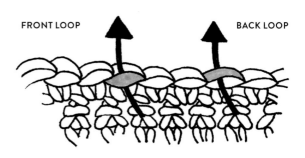

FRONT LOOP　　　　BACK LOOP

Working with multiple colours

JOINING A NEW COLOUR

When joining in a new colour at the beginning of a round or the middle of a row, work the last step of the stitch in the new colour. Catch the yarn in the new colour and draw through the loops on the hook to complete the stitch.

CARRYING UNUSED YARN ACROSS THE WORK

When the colour that is not in use is to be carried across the wrong side of the work, it can be hidden along the line of stitches being made by working over the unused strand every few stitches with the new colour. This method is used for the Dachshund and Spaniel's faces on pages 20 and 90. Lay the strand not being used on top of the previous row of stitches and crochet over it in the new colour, covering the unused colour.

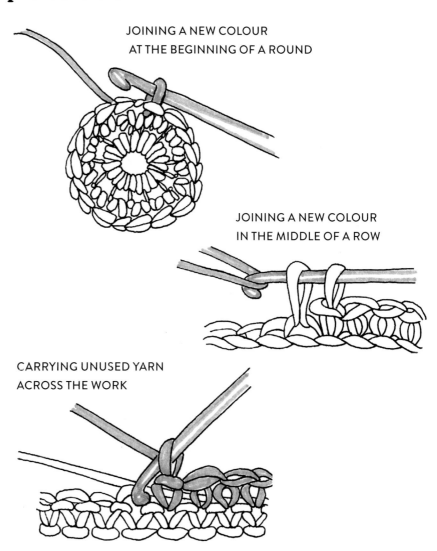

JOINING A NEW COLOUR AT THE BEGINNING OF A ROUND

JOINING A NEW COLOUR IN THE MIDDLE OF A ROW

CARRYING UNUSED YARN ACROSS THE WORK

Finishing Touches

HERE IS A GUIDE TO STUFFING AND SEWING THE PIECES TOGETHER, AND FINISHING THE DOGS WITH EMBROIDERED DETAILS AND TASSELS TO CREATE A LONG COAT.

Stuffing

Polyester stuffing is a synthetic fibre that is lightweight and washable. It can also be found in black, which won't be so visible through the crocheted fabric in darker shades of yarn. Pure wool stuffing is a lovely, natural fibre. Durable and soft, it can be washed by hand but cannot be machine-washed as it will shrink and felt. Kapok is a natural fibre with a soft, silky texture. It comes from a seedpod that is harvested from the Ceiba tree.

Before stuffing your dog, tease the fibres by pulling them apart with your fingers to make them light and fluffy. Use small amounts at a time and line the inside of the crocheted fabric with a layer of stuffing before building up the filling in the centre. This will prevent the crocheted piece from looking lumpy.

Sewing the pieces together

When stitching up your work, use glass-headed dressmakers' pins to hold the pieces together. To join the legs to the body, flatten the tops and pin in position. Insert the needle through one stitch of the body, then through a stitch of the leg. Insert the needle into the body, a little further along, then into the leg again and draw up the yarn tightly. Work around the top of the thigh and under the body to attach the leg securely.

BACK STITCH

This is a good method for sewing the dog's head to the body and attaching the ears and tail. Work close to the edges of the pieces for a neat finish.

Begin by working a couple of stitches over each other to secure the seam. Bring the needle through to the front of the work one stitch ahead of the last stitch made. Then insert the needle back through the work at the end of the last stitch. Repeat to complete the seam, making sure your stitches are neat.

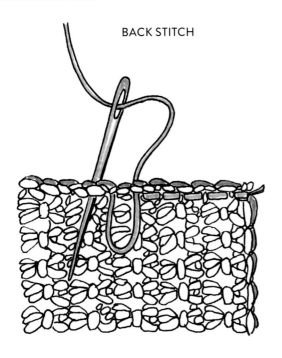

BACK STITCH

WHIP STITCH

Whip stitch is used to sew together the edges of most of the dogs' tails. Thread the tail of yarn left after fastening off onto a blunt-ended yarn needle. With wrong sides of the tail together, insert the needle from back to front through a stitch on both sides at the same time and draw the yarn through the stitch. Insert the needle through the next stitch on both sides from back to front as before and continue to the end. The yarn will be wrapped around the edges, joining the two sides.

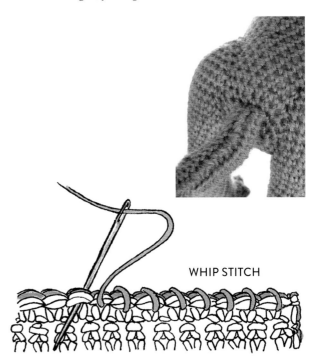

WHIP STITCH

Embroidery stitches

Embroidered stitches are used to add the features and markings. The eyes and noses are embroidered in satin stitch and the V-shaped crocheted stitches are followed to produce the colouring on the Spaniel's muzzle (see page 99).

STRAIGHT STITCH

This is a single stitch that can be worked in varying lengths, useful for embroidering lines.

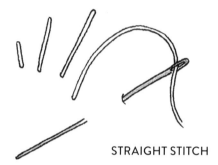

STRAIGHT STITCH

SATIN STITCH

Work straight stitches side by side and close together across a shape. Take care to keep the stitches even and the edge neat. The finished result will look like satin.

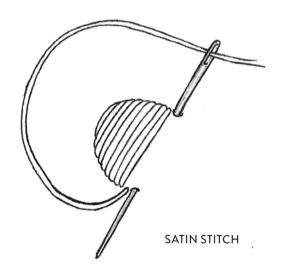

SATIN STITCH

SPANIEL'S MUZZLE MARKINGS

1 Insert the needle from the back to the front of the work at the base of the 'V' formed by the crocheted stitch that you want to embroider over. At the front of the work, insert the needle behind the top of the stitch and pull the yarn through.

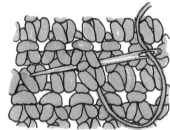

2 Insert the needle back through the point where it first emerged to cover the crocheted stitch.

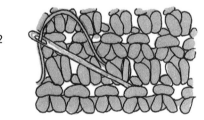

FASTENING OFF

To fasten off embroidery on the head or body, make a small knot in an area of the same colour where it won't show, or hide it where two pieces are joined, such as under the seam of the ear or behind the top of a leg. Weave in the ends of yarn.

Tassels

Tassels are used to create the long coat of the Yorkshire Terrier (see page 109) and the whiskers on the Border Terrier (see page 39). The strands of yarn can be trimmed to style.

To attach the tassel, fold the length of yarn in half to form a loop.

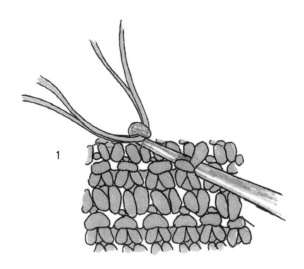

1 Insert the crochet hook behind the post of the stitch and back out through to the front. Catch the looped yarn and pull it a little way through.

2 Remove the hook and thread the ends of the yarn back through the loop, pulling them tight. This completes one tassel.

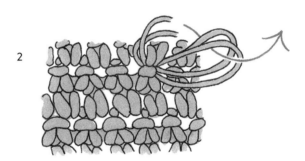

Abbreviations

ch chain

cm centimetre(s)

dc double crochet

dc2inc work 2 double crochet stitches into the next stitch to increase

dc2tog work 2 double crochet stitches together to decrease

dc3inc work 3 double crochet stitches into the next stitch to increase

dec decrease

htr half treble

in inch(es)

inc increase

lp st loop stitch

m metre(s)

mb make bobble

mm millimetre(s)

rep repeat

RS right side

sl st slip stitch

sp space

st(s) stitch(es)

tog together

tr treble

WS wrong side

yd yard(s)

yrh yarn round hook

Conversions

Steel crochet hooks

UK	Metric	US
6	0.60mm	14
5½	–	13
5	0.75mm	12
4½	–	11
4	1.00mm	10
3½	–	9
3	1.25mm	8
2½	1.50mm	7
2	1.75mm	6
1½	–	5

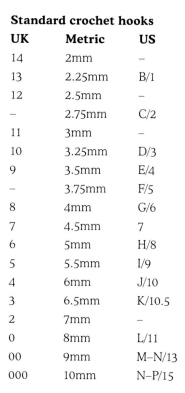

Standard crochet hooks

UK	Metric	US
14	2mm	–
13	2.25mm	B/1
12	2.5mm	–
–	2.75mm	C/2
11	3mm	–
10	3.25mm	D/3
9	3.5mm	E/4
–	3.75mm	F/5
8	4mm	G/6
7	4.5mm	7
6	5mm	H/8
5	5.5mm	I/9
4	6mm	J/10
3	6.5mm	K/10.5
2	7mm	–
0	8mm	L/11
00	9mm	M–N/13
000	10mm	N–P/15

UK/US crochet terms

UK	US
Double crochet	Single crochet
Half treble	Half double crochet
Treble	Double crochet

Note:
This book uses UK crochet terms

Suppliers

YARN

CANADA

Cascade Yarns
www.cascadeyarns.com

NORWAY

Drops Design
Drops Design A/S,
Jerikoveien 10 A
1067 Oslo
Tel: +47 23 30 32 20
www.garnstudio.com

UK

Deramores
Unit 1
Sabre Way
Peterborough
Cambridgeshire
PE1 5EJß
Tel: 0845 519 4573
Tel: +44 (0)1733 777345
www.deramores.com

King Cole Ltd
Merrie Mills
Snaygill Industrial Estate
Keighley Road
Skipton
North Yorkshire
BD23 2QR
Tel: +44 (0)1756 703670
www.kingcole.co.uk

Loveknitting Ltd
8th Floor
Aviation House
125 Kingsway
London
WC2B 6NH
Tel: +44 (0)1409 404010
www.lovecrafts.com

Patons
MEZ Crafts UK
17F Brooke's Mill
Armitage Bridge
Huddersfield
West Yorkshire
HD4 7NR
Tel: +44 (0)1484 668200
www.knitpatons.com

Rowan
MEZ Crafts UK
17F Brooke's Mill
Armitage Bridge
Huddersfield
West Yorkshire
HD4 7NR
Tel: +44 (0)1484 668200
www.knitrowan.com

Stylecraft
Spectrum Yarns
Spa Mill
Slaithwaite
Huddersfield
West Yorkshire
HD7 5BB
Tel: +44 (0)1484 848435
www.stylecraft-yarns.co.uk

The Stitchery
12–14 Riverside
Cliffe Bridge
High Street
Lewes
East Sussex
BN7 2RE
Tel: +44 (0)1273 473577
www.the-stitchery.co.uk

Wool Warehouse
12 Longfield Road
Sydenham Industrial Estate
Leamington Spa
Warwickshire
CV31 1XB
Tel: +44 (0)1926 882818
    0800 505 3300
www.woolwarehouse.co.uk

USA

Purl Soho
459 Broome Street
New York, NY 10013
Tel: +1 212 420 8796
www.purlsoho.com

CROCHET HOOKS

UK

Loveknitting Ltd
(see under Yarn)

The Stitchery
(see under Yarn)

Wool Warehouse
(see under Yarn)

USA
Purl Soho
(see under Yarn)

WADDING & TOY STUFFING

UK

Deramores
(see under Yarn)

Loveknitting Ltd
(see under Yarn)

Wool Warehouse
(see under Yarn)

World of Wool
Unit 8
The Old Railway Goods Yard
Scar Lane
Milnsbridge
Huddersfield
West Yorkshire
HD3 4PE
Tel: +44 (0)1484 846878
www.worldofwool.co.uk

USA

Purl Soho
(see under Yarn)

EMBROIDERY THREAD

UK

Hobbycraft
Customer Services
Hobbycraft DC
E-Commerce Door A
Parkway
Centrum 100 Business Park, Unit 1
Burton Upon Trent
DE14 2WA
Tel: +44 (0)330 026 1400
www.hobbycraft.co.uk

DMC Creative World
DMC Creative World Ltd
Unit 21
Warren Park Way
Warren Park
Enderby
Leicester
LE19 4SA
Tel: +44 (0)1924 371501
www.dmc.com

Index

First published 2020 by Guild of Master Craftsman Publications Ltd,
Castle Place, 166 High Street, Lewes, East Sussex, BN7 1XU, UK.

Text and designs © Vanessa Mooncie, 2020
Copyright in the Work © GMC Publications Ltd, 2020

ISBN 978 1 78494 566 4
All rights reserved

While every effort has been made to obtain permission from the
copyright holders for all material used in this book, the publishers
will be pleased to hear from anyone who has not been appropriately
acknowledged and to make the correction in future reprints.

The publishers and author can accept no legal responsibility for
any consequences arising from the application of information,
advice or instructions given in this publication.

A catalogue record for this book is available from the British Library.

PUBLISHER: Jonathan Bailey
PRODUCTION: Jim Bulley and Jo Pallett
SENIOR PROJECT EDITOR: Wendy McAngus
MANAGING ART EDITOR: Gilda Pacitti
EDITOR: Nicola Hodgson
DESIGN & ART DIRECTION: Wayne Blades
PHOTOGRAPHER: Neal Grundy
PATTERN CHECKING: Jude Roust
ILLUSTRATIONS & CHARTS: Vanessa Mooncie

Colour origination by GMC Reprographics
Printed and bound in China

Acknowledgements

I thank Jonathan Bailey for giving me the opportunity to write *Crocheted Dogs*. Thank you to Wendy McAngus and all at GMC, Wayne Blades and Neal Grundy. I dedicate this book to Dolly, Leo and Winter, who always take an interest in what I am making, particularly when it's something they can play with.

To order a book,
or to request a catalogue,
contact:

GMC Publications Ltd
Castle Place, 166 High Street,
Lewes, East Sussex,
BN7 1XU
United Kingdom
Tel: +44 (0)1273 488005
www.gmcbooks.com